PARFUMS

A CATALOGUE OF
REMEMBERED SMELLS

Philippe Claudel

PARFUMS

A CATALOGUE OF
REMEMBERED SMELLS

Translated from the French by
Euan Cameron

MACLEHOSE PRESS
QUERCUS · LONDON

First published in the French language as *Parfums*
by Éditions Stock, Paris, in 2012
First published in Great Britain in 2014
This paperback edition published in 2015 by

MacLehose Press
an imprint of Quercus
Carmelite House
50 Victoria Embankment
London EC4Y 0DZ

An Hachette Company

This book has been selected to receive financial assistance from English PEN's PEN
Translates! programme. English PEN exists to promote literature and our understanding
of it, to uphold writers' freedoms around the world, to campaign against the persecution
and imprisonment of writers for stating their views, and to promote the friendly
co-operation of writers and the free exchange of ideas.
www.englishpen.org

A CIP catalogue record for this book is available from the British Library.

ISBN (MMP) 978 1 78206 616 3
ISBN (Ebook) 978 1 782066 15 6

10 9 8 7 6 5 4 3 2 1

Designed and typeset in Quadraat by Libanus Press, Marlborough
Printed and bound in Great Britain by Clays Ltd, St Ives plc

For my friend Jean-Marc,
to our shared path,
past, present and to come

Let me breathe in the fragrance of your hair
for a long, long time, bury my entire face in it,
as a thirsty man in the water of a spring,
and ruffle it with my hand like a scented handkerchief,
so as to scatter the memories in the air.

CHARLES BAUDELAIRE
Un Hémisphère dans une chevelure

CONTENTS

Acacia

A CLIMATIC INCONGRUITY: I HAVE SEEN TREES covered in snow in early June. Clusters of fluffy snow, thick and light at the same time, which the evening breeze skims as one might caress a loved one's belly. I'm speeding along on a bicycle down the narrow lane that dips behind the cemetery in Dombasle, the town where I was born, the town of my childhood, still my town today, towards the old Sommerviller stadium where we play our games. Rough-and-tumble games, ball games, cops and robbers. I'm going to meet my pals: Noche, the Waguette twins, Eric Chochnaki, Denis Paul, Jean-Marc Cesari, Francis Del Fabro, Didier Simonin, Didier Faux, Jean-Marie Arnould, Petitjean, Marc Jonet. The tall acacia trees shield the bright sky and bend together in an ornate canopy. Leaves the shape of ancient coins. Crowns of thorns for absent victims. I pedal with my eyes closed and I toss my head back, drunk with the fragrance of the petals and the feverish joy that returns every spring. The days shall stretch out endlessly, like our lives. We shall await the evening amid the renewed sounds of birds and frogs. We shall be astonished by the grip of the earth's last chill, and refreshed by it. Even the mists will set off on a journey, far away, and not return until October. The sky will give birth to pink sunsets, swathed in orange and pale blue as in the paintings of Claude Gellée, known as le Lorrain, who was a born a few miles away three centuries earlier. The honey and primrose-scented acacia blossom buzzes with bees that reel about intoxicated in the soft air like tiny, downy campion flowers. The rest of us, small human creatures, search among the lowest branches for the heavy clumps with their pale cream hue. We pick them, heedless of the grazes to our fingers and wrists, and our beads of blood reveal our bravery. I clasp the freshly cut young bunches in a cloth and return home, pedalling for all I'm worth. I pass the drowsy, listless abattoirs where the flayed cattle, suspended from their hooks in the cold storage rooms, contemplate their brief fate. My mother has beaten the batter. We toss in the acacia clusters which grow heavy with a pale magma. Then, very quickly, they have to be thrown in the boiling oil so that their rich smell does not die but is trapped beneath the thin crust. Golden-brown. Outside, the night has opened wide her Prussian-blue eye. The cat beside the stove observes us and wonders. It's late. It's early. Eyes gleaming, ignoring my burning lips, I bite into a crispy cluster brimming with flowers, smiles and the breeze. The very essence of spring is there in my mouth.

Garlic

FIRST OF ALL, THE KNIFE CARVES A NOTCH IN THE
clove. A knife with a blade that looks like a very thin crescent
moon so much has it been sharpened. It is the same knife that
my grandmother – whom we nickname the Flea in spite of her
plump girth – uses, in my presence, without any qualms and
with a precise motion, to thrust into the throats of rabbits to
make the blood spew out, and I never avert my eyes, preferring
this honest means of slaughter to the hypocritical use of a
bludgeon that some people employ. My father goes about it in
the same way. I never miss a single execution. I particularly like
the moment when, having made small slits around the paws,
he swiftly turns the skin inside out, like a sock, and detaches
it from the bluish ivory of the body. The naked clove of the
garlic resembles the canine tooth of a big cat, and the weapon
used for the crime chisels out of it tiny, pearly, slightly greasy
cubes that scarcely have time to give off their aromas because
my grandmother throws them promptly into the dented, black

frying pan, over the steak that is already sizzling. Explosion. Smoke from a blacksmith's forge. Eyes smarting. The kitchen of the small house at 18 rue des Champs Fleury disappears in billows of fumes. My mouth waters. The smell of garlic, of burning butter, of blood and fluids, is converted into a delicious juice from the meat as it merges with the melting fat. Hollow with hunger, I wait. At table. Knife and fork at the ready. A white cloth tied around my neck. My feet do not yet touch the ground. I am Tom Thumb, but I'm becoming the Ogre. I have a lifetime ahead of me. Grandmère opens a window giving onto the courtyard to usher out the food-stall smell and places on my repaired earthenware plate, with the worn and crackled hunting-scene design that I love, the steak that we went to buy that very morning at Petit Maire's, the butcher's on rue Carnot. The cubes of garlic have shrivelled. Some have turned reddish-brown, some sepia, others have a caramel tinge while some, astonishingly, have retained their jasmine colour. They all diffuse their intangible miracle over the hot, golden meat. Grandmother completes her task by delicately trimming a little parsley with her black dressmaker's scissors so that it is sprinkled over the meat, giving it a fragrance of fresh grass, then she looks at me and smiles. "Aren't you going to eat?" I ask her. "Watching you eat is my food," she replies. She died when I was eight years old.

Still

IT'S A DR MABUSE HUT, MADE OF ROUGHLY CUT wooden planks, poorly spliced, blackened in places as though charred by stubborn flames over time. It stands above the River Sânon, near the Pierre Escuras bridge, hanging over the edge, and secured to the steep bank by some miraculous attachment or other. Beneath it, the wintry waters, sparse, grey and murky, the trails of algae like grimy hair, and not very far away the harbour on the Grand Canal where the barges moor, side by side, like large fish with their bellies stuffed with limestone and coal. In January, the hut awakes from its slumber. You are aware of hissing sounds, indefinable noises, the drip-drip of gurgling fluids, but sometimes, too, a cough or a song, a whistled tune, a swear-word or two. As children, we hang around in the vicinity, our throats and nostrils open wide, breathing in everything given off by these walls until our chests are ready to burst, untroubled by the cold that makes our fingers numb and our cheeks ruddy. The invisible still, and its owner whom we never see either, draw us like moths teetering around an alcoholic sun. Because there, in the depths of a mystery we do not understand, it is actually the sun that, in the twists and coils of the labyrinth of heated copper, turns itself into *eau de vie*. A sun of gold and mauve fruits – mirabelles, pears, quetsches, wild sloes – gathered a few months earlier from beneath the trees and so ripe that their sugary weight has often caused them to fall and split, under the weight of their profusion and baked flesh; the fruit is then mixed together in casks and, instead of rotting, is blended into a heady and fizzy must. The final act is played out in the hut above the river. The flesh becomes pure alcohol. The machine releases the liquid into the bottles and demijohns brought by our fathers, but it also provides the angels with their share, which the rickety hut magnanimously allows to soar upwards. In heaven they are probably drunk on these vapours, but on earth, we, who are no longer angels and not yet demons, become, thanks to them, dazed fauns zigzagging along on our bikes, laughing for no reason, happy, intoxicated by this flurry of alcohol and life.

Girlfriends

SO WHAT IS THIS FRAGRANCE OUR PETITES AMOUREUSES, our first girlfriends, have, when our lips initially find theirs for the first time, and then, awkwardly, don't really know what to do? I am twelve years old. Girls don't look at me and boys tease me for being skinny. My over-eager heart beats madly whenever dark-haired Natalie or blonde Valérie walk past me. I write poems that I slip into their hands at eight o'clock in the morning when I arrive at the Collège Julienne Farenc. Cleopatra, Helen of Troy, Athene, Aphrodite, Diana, Nefertiti: I recycle the history and mythology syllabus. And, shamelessly, I plunder the authors in our French textbook: *Valérie, sous le Pont des Voleurs coule le Sânon, Et mes amours, Faut-il qu'il m'en souvienne* or else *Demain dès l'aube, à l'heure où blanchit la campagne, je partirai à l'école Nathalie, je sais que tu m'attends, je ne puis demeurer loin de toi plus longtemps.* But Nathalie does not wait for me. As though to prove the intensity of my passion, I invent, in honour of Valérie, the verb *radadorer*, the repetitive superlative of "to adore". Valérie,

17

je te radadore! All I am allowed in return is a shrug and a disdain-
ful pout. My poems end up as scrunched-up balls of paper in the
gutter. They're thrown there right in front of me. To be sprayed
on by dogs and cats. Playing the role of the sentry, that's all
I'm good at, warning François, who is kissing Nathalie, or
Denis, who is doing the same with Valérie, whenever an adult
approaches and they risk being caught in the act in the narrow
alleyways that connect rue Jules Ferry to rue Jeanne d'Arc.
I'm the willing little sucker cuckold, keeping watch over the
love affairs that others are having with my girlfriends. I ask
them afterwards what they taste like and smell of, these kisses
mimicking those that can be seen every Sunday on the screen of
the Georges cinema, film kisses that are as ardent as they are
motionless, and which could pass as advertisements for super-
glue. They call them *patins*. But the only *patins* I know are the
slippers we wear at home to polish the floors. They're old, with
a tartan design, and they stink. A few months later, I learn how
it's done: it won't be with either Nathalie or Valérie, but with
Christine Frenzi. Fat Frenzi. A birthday tea party at the Waguette
twins. We eat cake. We drink Sic orangeade and Sic lemonade
with psychedelic colours. Someone puts on some music; it's
slow, easy-listening stuff, as syrupy as the drinks. Couples team
up. They shuffle around as best they can. Many of the dancers
are in shorts. There are only two people still sitting down, her
and me. She comes to fetch me, she takes me by the hand. I dare
not refuse, and here I am pressed up against her. My arms can
barely reach round her body. I feel slightly ashamed. What will
Nathalie and Valérie think, both draped over my friends, so

near, yet so far away? I close my eyes. It is she, too, who puts her face against mine, who seeks out my lips, finds them, kisses them. Silky hair washed in the same Dop shampoo as mine, but smelling of something else too – something vegetable and sugary, candied, a whiff of confectionery, of home-made cakes, of plant stems and open fields – that I can't identify, but which takes hold of me and which I breathe in happily, on her neck, on her lips, those lips that I kiss again, and this time I'm the one who wants it. Nathalie is forgotten, Valérie is forgotten. Their loss. And when, after the dance, Fat Frenzi does what the other girls have done with the boys and comes to sit on my lap, and the pain crushes my bare thighs and the few muscles I have on my bones, I say nothing. I grit my teeth. I inhale her neck, her cheeks, her mouth. We kiss again and for years afterwards these kisses, which are scented with the green smell of angelica – at last I've succeeded in naming it – impel me to go and open the jar of crystallised fruit which my mother uses to make cakes and decorate rum babas and which she keeps in the bottom of the kitchen cupboard. I grab a handful of sticks of this sweet and sticky candied umbellifer, pass them under my nose, close my eyes, and munch them as I sit on the linoleum floor, thinking of Fat Frenzi and her kisses – but also of Michèle Mercier, whose delicately erotic adventures are shown on television each summer – while at the same time humming the sickly sweet tune that brought us together: *On ira, où tu voudras quand tu voudras, et l'on s'aimera encore, lorsque l'amour sera mort.* Thanks be to Joe Dassin for having helped me far more than Apollinaire and Hugo combined ever did.

Aftershave

I LOOK UP AT MY FATHER FROM A DIRECT, LOW-angled viewpoint. We are in the cellar of the house, in the shower room. He is standing over the washbasin in front of a small cupboard attached to the wall with three mirrored doors. By adjusting them, the triptych enables you to look at three faces instead of one, and sometimes even more. The electric razor glides over his skin which he stretches with his fingers so as to keep it flat. He glides over the same places several times, eventually leaving a complexion that is both smooth and mottled with reddish patches. Beneath my steady gaze, my father gradually becomes younger. The night's beard disappears, white or grey, ash that has settled on his face during his sleep to make him older and steal him from me. The music of the razor is a psalmody. A prayer consisting of just two or three notes and a *basso continuo* that is like the monotonous chant of certain muezzins. It is always dank in the shower room. The smell of Turkish baths once the heat has gone. Of swimming pool changing rooms. The room has no window. To ventilate it, you have to open two doors, one after the other, the one to the laundry room and the one to the summer kitchen. My father unplugs the razor, gathers up its cord, places both in the left-hand compartment of the bathroom cupboard, and takes out a large, flat bottle filled with a kind of green water. *Mennen, pour nous les hommes.* I am far from being a man. By shaking the bottle, he lets a spray spurt out into the open hollow of his left hand. As in the advertisements. Very quickly, he dabs his cheeks, his chin and his neck several times with the palm of his now moistened hand. We are assaulted by superior scents of menthol and citrus, made all the more intense by the presence of alcohol that swirls in the air and stings our nostrils. But it fades. All that remains is a fragrance that is reminiscent of balm and of lemon, of the garden mint I sometimes like to chew, of emerald leaves and pale tisane, yellow rind and pepper too. My father, who refers to me as Nonome, or Julot, bends down towards me. He offers me his burning cheeks, which I kiss. A ritual. They have grown strangely supple and tender, with a softness that has lost all masculinity. My father, through the miracle of shaving and green water, has become a tiny baby again.

Party-time

EVEN THOUGH THE BRIGHT DAYLIGHT OUTSIDE
bleaches the walls white, what we need is darkness. Artificial.
Darkness conjured up from nowhere by whatever means at
our disposal. We are young, barely sixteen, and we are already
burying ourselves. In cellars. In broken-down sheds. In garages
with their windows covered by tarpaulins. Searching for dark
recesses, hidden corners, sofas sufficiently battered that we
can use their armrests as shields. Hiding away from others.
Hiding away from ourselves, from our fear of a girl coming
near, of feeling her right there, pressed to us, trying to slip
our hand onto her hip, on her breasts, searching for her lips
without her seeing the acne on our left cheek that is about
to burst. Not let her see anything. And not let anything be
seen. Not hear anything either, so that when we say "I love
you", the words are smothered beneath the decibels of MC5,
the Ramones, Patti Smith, Téléphone, Trust, Clash or the Sex
Pistols. We can always pretend afterwards that we never uttered

them. We're blind. Deaf. Dumb, or virtually so. With a craving in our bellies which gnaws at our guts – shall I dare, shall I not dare – and which the first alcoholic drinks struggle to quell. And then dancing, contorting our bodies, rhythmically or not, exhausting ourselves dancing so as not to explode from all that energy that groans within us, that tingles inside us, and then to release our sweat, our moods, our anger, in the shady room that is becoming suffocating. And it's so good to suffocate, to feel on ourselves that bitter, animal, adolescent heat of T-shirts and shirts that cling to our skins, that are enmeshed in the fog of cigarettes, the whiff of yeast and hops. Our young bodies, surrounded by the perfumes of girls who are made up like Nina Hagen, Kate Bush or Lene Lovich, of boys' deodorants, of sweet-smelling mouths, with the occasional hint of engine oil, petrol cans, lubricant, engine grease and white spirit that escapes from the garage. Hours spent like this, unsettled ones, in those chiselled-down, bare, hollow Giscard years, beside the great chasm of life into which, like little *bombes humaines*, we hope to cast ourselves, without knowing anything about it, wild, uncontrollable and quite unconcerned, awash with dreams and love, spewing out our beers and the adult world. And later on, staggering around, head splitting from music and alcohol, red-eyed, retrieving everything on our clammy shirts that we remove once we get home, stained, drink-sodden, smoke-filled, kissed, worn out, limp, still damp. Like our lips and our hearts.

Mist

SLEEPING HORSES ALWAYS LOOK LIKE LARGE corpses. Lying on their sides, legs outstretched, they seem to be waiting for the knacker's cart that will haul them off to the pit to be carved up. Partly shrouding them, the mist makes them seem eerie. I go through Saint-Nicolas-de-Port whose tall basilica breaks through the mist, dabbing its white walls with rays of rather pale sunshine. I think of the cavalry soldiers during the Thirty Years' War, of Jacques Callot's hanged men, of the animals and humans devoured by wolves during the long winters, of Raymond Schwab's fine novel, *Mengeatte*, recommended to me by Roland Clément, poet and librarian, who with his wife ran Le Tour du Monde bookshop in rue des Michottes, in Nancy, when I was a student. Horses and mist together therefore all along the road that leads me to Rosières-aux-Salines. I pedal gently. The less time I have, the longer I take. The mist acts like the lid of a casserole dish: it preserves within it, beneath it, the smell of earth caught unaware by an early autumn, of grass sapped by the morning chill, of animals still out in the meadows, of empty fields and sodden asphalt. It's like a large bottle without an exterior, a never-ending spray. While they watch, I inhale the horses' hides, their heavy breathing soothed by sleep, their flanks smeared with dung. And I am reminded of other horses: they, too, emerge from the mist as though from a strange romantic dream. They are Ardennais, Percherons, Boulonnais, their coats beaded with moisture. Harnessed in pairs, they haul the low barges along the towpath. I am a child. Their breath casts up clouds and, when I pass alongside them, I can feel the great heat of these toiling creatures, their taut, steaming muscles and sappy coats. I always like the mist because it enables me to enter into my innermost being. Walking out of doors, in a landscape that only reveals its immediate fringes to me, even though they are already swallowed up by the erasing of an invisible rubber, the world becomes a simple projection of the soul, a pervasive and slightly chilling assumption. I am alone. Intimately alone, and I recoil into this thought as a snail does into its shell. In the opaque presence of the mist, barely broken here and there, according to some inscrutable logic, by tints of whiteness that make you think that there are sources of light further away, there is the unexpected advent of a benign apocalypse, one without major repercussions and pain. A dispassionate extractor of suspended and dormant scents, the mist disrupts the day-to-day landscape so that it may be seen and experienced differently. So it is that rue Hélène, which begins almost opposite my house, and which normally offers the prospect

25

of a narrow row of workers' cottages – small, simple and unadorned, the unoccupied houses dying, with their closed shutters and barren little gardens, with a short alleyway that slopes towards the wall of the Casino assembly room and its bandstand – takes on in foggy weather an atmosphere of Flemish mystery. One that releases the fragrances from the moss-covered tiles and exudes coke, moisture, rope, woollen overcoats and river breezes – those from the Sânon, which is not far away, but also those from the two nearby canals, le Petit and le Grand – and you smell them here as much as you see them, just as you imagine them as much as you experience them. Simenon is here, and his whole universe looms up in the smoke from the red glow of a pipe which a lost walker lights up twenty yards away as he disappears in the mist, under the mandorla of a dim lamplight beneath which a dog, a plump mongrel with tired teats, eventually pisses while yapping half-heartedly.

Cannabis

I'M NOT SOMEONE WHO SMOKES JOINTS. I ROLL them for others. I like handiwork. The precise movements, the techniques, the human ingenuity that consists in using basic materials – a few cigarette papers, a scrap of cardboard, some tobacco and some hemp, a little saliva – to produce something that is efficient and simple to use. In the same way, I admire the know-how and resourcefulness of a friend, Ben, who lives in Nancy with his partner Nanou on the unheated top floor of a building in rue Gustave Simon. In the adjoining loft, during the summer season, Ben grows a miniature forest of Indian hemp, tending it with the care of an amateur horticulturalist who subscribes to *Rustica*. Nanou and Ben belong to another age. It is 1983, and even though they listen to the Cure, U2, Joy Division, the Stranglers or Depeche Mode, their hairstyles – long, smooth and sober – their Citroën 2C.V.s, their large, hand-knitted sweaters that reach down to their knees, the mere fact of their being an established couple when neither of them is more than twenty-two years old are all proof that they are two or three decades out of date or ahead of their time; as are their passions for the Meuse and the Ardèche, organic food, bulgur wheat, sprouting cress, their loathing of nuclear energy and pesticides, their admiration for leading environmentalists who at the time don't yet have much to get excited about, their sabotaging of the E.D.F. electricity meter with the help of a simple Bic biro. You drink a lot at their place. You smoke even more. This produces sluggish conversations during which Ben likes to don a C.R.S. riot police helmet stolen by his brother-in-law Patrick, a progressive French teacher, during a demonstration on the Larzac plateau. Sentences are begun, but rarely completed. Movements are slow, the eyes heavy and dazed. Even kisses die on lips that are attempting to come together. Everybody is everyone else's friend. The soft strains of Mark Knopfler's guitar accompany the fumes rising to the skies. Even though I am not a user, I inhale so much cannabis, whose scent of herbs, dead grass, burned fallow land, natural medicine and dry wood I adore, that I don't come away unscathed. The world starts to resemble a universe of flabby monsters. The pieces of furniture become soft and springy and join in the discussions. The lights dance just like Nanou who, standing on a low table, is absolutely determined to show us her breasts. The kilim concealing a number of missing wooden floorboards undulates like the spine of some very supple animal. The girl beside me thinks that my name is Jean-Luc. I try to persuade her to take her clothes off, but she replies that she can only make love to Jean-Pauls. Occasionally, nowadays, standing near a bus stop, in the vicinity of a school, in a porch way, I catch a whiff of grass. In the blink of an eyelid I am back at Ben and Nanou's. I am in their home, in their attic, feet on the table, a glass of Gordon's beside me. I am listening distractedly to Ben telling me that cheeses with a cooked crust are carcinogenic and that François Mitterrand, under the guise of being a left-wing president, will eventually fuck us all up, while I, by way of paying my share as a guest, roll a perfect joint for him. Nearby, on the gas cooker, the bulgur wheat and tomato sauce bubble away. Nanou is singing "Sunday Bloody Sunday" at the top of her voice as she stirs the pot so it doesn't stick. It doesn't feel very cold yet. I really think I'm happy.

Cinnamon

I GREW UP IN A LAND OF SHARPLY CONTRASTED seasons, abrupt and absolute. And winter, which brings the years to an end rather in the way one closes the door on a room glutted with gold and crystal, is not the least of these. We dream about it. We sing about it. We eat and we drink during it. These December feasts and refreshments washed down with the wines of Alsace, Gewürztraminer and Riesling, and *eaux-de-vies* made from pears, plums or raspberries, will not really come to an end until Candlemas, in a swirl of warm crêpes. Cinnamon is the exotic guest. It is scarcely used during the rest of the year, other than in stewed apples from time to time or, in late August, on a *tarte aux quetsches*. When the first chills arrive, it shows its spicy face. Sticks resembling parchments that have caught fire and curled in on themselves are taken out of large glass jars. They are ground to a powder in a mortar. A present from the Three Wise Men. The Orient settles itself into the kitchens, bringing with it its retinue and its mirages which it pours out over the Formica furniture and the old waxed tablecloth. Shortbread biscuits, cakes, rolls, brioches, linzertortes, kugelhopfs, all are sprinkled with cinnamon and metamorphosed by it. Cookery allows us to immerse ourselves in Europe and in the past, greedy, flour-speckled travellers that we are. For years I have wanted to draw up a geographical map of the strudel – that delicate confection rolled in flaky pastry, with apples and raisins in its most authentic version – one which delineates, more or less, the frontiers of the old Austro-Hungarian Empire, since it can be enjoyed just as much in Vienna, Venice, Trieste, Bucharest, Warsaw, Prague, Budapest or Brno, but equally in New York where so many of the emigrants from the ruins and the ashes came to hope in life again. To tell the truth, it's the cinnamon in this patisserie that haunts me, its heady olfactory music of winter and holidays, a legal narcotic capable of making even the most French of pastries refined and elegant, giving them genuine flavour. Even ordinary red wine, if allowed to simmer for a long time in a saucepan at the back of the stove, and after tossing in some sugar, a slice of orange, a clove and a pinch of cinnamon, is transformed into a diabolically bewitching concoction that burns the hand holding the glass in which it is served. It warms the mouth, the throat, puts fire in the belly, and provokes laughter, lights up the eye and jovial cheeks reddened by the cold outside. Tongues start to spin stories and fantasies. Memories are shuffled – those from life, those from History, and those from novels – like a pack of cards. All of a sudden, people start talking of minarets, of the tundra and of princesses locked away. Of caravanserais, miniature horses and steppes. Of coarse tobacco, shattered swords, of the Emperor in his chilly castle, of frozen leather and soldiers who have remained loyal, drowned in a Russian sea, even though all is lost, the world has ended and they will never know.

Cellar

MY THIRION GREAT-AUNTS, MY PATERNAL GRAND-
mother's sisters, live in Saint-Blaise, a small, one-street village
in the Vosges. We call them "The Aunts from Saint-Blaise",
thus amalgamating them into one ancient triad and omitting
the first names that might differentiate them: Berthe, Catherine
and Marguerite. Why do I still retain in my memory today, in
an excessively precise way, their features, their wrinkles, their
hairstyles, their grey, black and blue-denim clothing? I still
love my maternal grandmother dearly and yet I have forgotten
her face. I don't much care for these unsmiling old women, yet
they have nevertheless established themselves quite comfort-
ably in my memories as if they were at home there. Never
having married, they live in the large family house, the back
roof of which abuts the kitchen garden where cabbages stand
guard until the first frosts have passed. Beyond it lies the
forest with its velvety jumble of dark fir trees, mosses and
low branches. They receive us in their kitchen, meanly lit by a

low window and a hanging lamp that is only switched on when you can no longer see anyone's face. I am surrounded by quarrels that elude me, the reasons for which are rooted in muddy resentment: a mirabelle tart, soft and tasteless and already half eaten, is offered to us each time, as if it were some sumptuous present. And to the great displeasure of my mother, who is a first-rate pastrycook, I devour it, which invariably leads one of the aunts to remark: "Well, the little fellow really was hungry!" – a way of reproaching my mother for not feeding me properly, and therefore being a neglectful mother. I am then allowed to wander around the house. I go upstairs into bedrooms last slept in by human beings in 1915. I open wardrobes, I come across bowler hats reeking of mothballs, dead men's suits, dainty bamboo walking sticks, bunches of dried flowers, coloured photographs. This museum of extinguished lives seems to me like a book without letters of the alphabet. I sense dimly that one day I shall have to collect them together and write it. The child that I am is allowed to breathe in these smells of dead pollen, widowed woollens and orphaned linen so that one day he can piece them together into a narrative and resurrect lives lost through wars, illnesses and accidents. The bedrooms, the lofts and the places high up become murmuring lamentations, whereas the cellar, the lower abdomen of this vast house, is a poem of the Underworld. I quake as I enter it, but I never reach the far end – is there one, in fact? After a few meters, the darkness becomes all-pervading. The racks that contain bottles of wine with dusty necks and cans of vegetables disappear, as does the stone vault.

The cold grows tangible and, as my feet leave the rock floor, I step onto earth that you would think had been turned over by a gravedigger's shovel. The cavern discharges its deep, pit-like breath over me, heavy, clinging, seeped in clay and mud. I shiver. I stop moving. I try to remain in the abyss for as long as possible. My heart, a small, caged animal, thumps against its fleshy bars. The cellar attempts to enchant me with its whiff of must and saltpetre, of muffled condensation, a siren from the depths with a night-time kiss that oppresses me and winds itself around me. But my overwhelming fear eventually gains the upper hand and I turn my back on the inky infinity, and rush down the narrow corridors into my mother's arms, panting hard, beneath the dry and disapproving glares of the three elderly aunts, two of whom are stroking their hairy chins as they grumble away.

Hotel rooms

I HAVE STAYED IN MANY HOTEL ROOMS. TOO MANY, no doubt. And what, as a child, put me in a wild state of excitement is now a source of harmless dread. Shall I like this hotel room to which I have just been given the key and which I know nothing about yet, neither its light, its colours, its furniture nor its smell? Shall I feel at ease there? And above all, especially, will I be able to write there? For over the years, hotel rooms have become my offices and my laboratories. They are where I bring forth my little stories. As well as in trains and planes. So whether stationary or on the move, I'm shut away, and always far from home. I am five, seven, ten years old. The hotel room means the holidays. It takes on responsibility for their duration and their unfamiliarity. Nothing there smells as it does at home, and what I remember with clarity is the scent of the soap and the hand-towels that greet me, the moment the door is opened, in those bedrooms in the Ötztal valley, in the Tyrol, with their simple decorations, varnished woodwork and quilted duvets, a foretaste of the sweet comfort in which I shall spend a few days. This room is not mine. It knows nothing about me and it won't retain anything of me. I enter it as I would a new place, with no memories of other people, a completely impersonal space that could make me feel ill at ease, but which, on the contrary, confirms my status as a traveller, as a human being in transit. We ought to read more into hotel rooms as metaphors of our lives. New carpets, linen laundered and ironed by industrial cleaning companies that all use the same efficient and odourless products – and that absence of smells eventually becomes one itself – disinfected bathroom, odourless wardrobes, occasionally flowers in vases, but flowers that deliberately have no scent and are unobtrusive, orchids usually. Only bathroom products offer fragrances. Shower gels, moisturiser, soap. I'll come back to that. And to those childhood impressions. The hotel room is somewhere you don't use the same soap you do at home. Sometimes, I don't write anything there. The place won't allow me to do so and I don't attempt to understand why. Occasionally, I write for hours, forgetting my own life and the passing of time. The space only belongs to me temporarily. I leave my scent there, as an animal does on a run or in undergrowth where it spends the night. But the following day, shortly after I leave, everything to do with me will have been wiped away. Nobody who goes into the bedroom will know that I have used it. We are very quickly forgotten there. Another metaphor. Now and then, bending down in search of spectacles or a pen I've just dropped, I find a sock, a button, a chewing-gum wrapper. Only then, because of these clues, do I become aware that the bedroom has known at least one other occupant whose existence is affirmed by these trivial things. But I am neither a policeman nor an archaeologist, and I cast these things aside without making them talk. In certain bedrooms, people have smoked. The stench of cold tobacco lingers, ingrained in the carpets and the net curtains, deep in bed-frames and mattresses, inside wardrobes. Soap and tobacco. A curious mixture, but all stale tobacco eventually comes to have the same stench. It tells you nothing about the person who has smoked it. Besides, is it a man or a woman? Who has actually slept here the previous night? A hotel bedroom has no gender. Or it could be a hermaphrodite. In fact, it couldn't care less. It couldn't give a damn. She gives herself to whoever pays. She's a whore who shuts her eyes and refuses to kiss. She weds us for a few hours, for a single night, makes us feel we're the only ones, she envelops herself in our exhalations the better to lie to us, and then discards them just as she discards us. Her true fragrance is that of our fleetingness, our inconsistency.

Coal

WE KEEP OURSELVES WARM WITH WOOD AND COAL.
More with coal than wood, actually, and before every winter
the lorry from Aubert's comes with its delivery. Dozens of
sacks, made of grubby jute, carried by two men with blackened
faces in which only the white of their teeth and their eyes
reveal any humanity, though a somewhat disturbing humanity:
that of a killer or someone who devours children. Like the
one with the name of the Nordic god, Odin. Their strangler's
hands grab hold of the sacks on the platform of the lorry, and,
heaving them onto their backs, they half balance them on
their shoulders before taking them down to the cellar at a
slow, regular pace. Once their task is done, they wipe the sweat
from their foreheads with the back of their dirty hands. My
father offers them a glass of red wine which they down in one,
on their feet, standing there without saying a word. Briquettes,
nuts, or else loose coal. The heap of coal is next to the heap
of potatoes. Both piles shrink simultaneously over the course

of weeks. The duration of the cold season can be measured accordingly. A dark, heavy smoke trickles from all the chimneys in town, and it struggles to rise up into the sky or to dissolve there. Frequently, the sky even rejects it and drives the smoke back towards the ground, towards us, in other words. We then choke on this asphyxiating fog with its particles of soot that are scattered everywhere, on gardens, over the clothes hung out to dry, in our hair, on the snow which in so doing meets its opposite. I am sent to do some shovelling. I fill the strange zinc bucket with its square base that narrows and curves at the top. I carry it upstairs, holding it with both hands. The furnace waits, like a starving animal expecting to be given its food. I raise the flap with a hook and roll the black substance into the glowing jaws. The excruciating heat scorches the skin and sometimes singes my eyebrows a little. The smell of roasting pig. The Sougland stove digests its portion. It starts to purr contentedly. Replete. I open my satchel and start to do my homework on the kitchen table surrounded by the aroma of the evening soup. I feel happy. I like to read and write in kitchens. For me it's the most important place, simple and unfussy, and far from all stuffy formality. One doesn't have to pretend or perform any social games there. The kitchen knows our innermost truths. It sees us in the mornings with our faces chewed over by the night, and in the evenings when, after too long a day, we lower our guard, unbuckle our belt and lay bare our frailties. Coal merchants gradually begin to disappear as central heating becomes more common. A revolution. We can keep warm without making a mess. Cellars are no longer black with soot. Housewives don't have to tidy up the dust. Chimneys only emit transparent wafts that no longer smell of anything. The smell is forgotten. The mines are closed. The pitheads are sealed off. Coal slowly disappears from our lives. Many years later, I am walking through the streets of a city in Poland. Katowice. It's February. It's very cold. Night has already fallen. I stroll past well-padded figures on the pavements, walking quickly, their heads bowed and hidden under large caps and hats with ear-flaps. Shops are badly lit. Unappealing cafés. A few drunkards are squabbling with their shadows. And then all of a sudden, with a sharp gust of wind that has blown down from on high and has swept off the roofs anything that could be languishing there, here I am in a fog of grimy, acrid smoke, slightly green or yellow, irritating my throat and nose. Coal. Coal that is still burned here and around these parts, in this landscape of working mines. A smell of childhood and a smell of poverty, one of sadness too, as though the black, combusted particles were illustrations of the misfortunes, great or small, harmful or benign, enduring or passing, that settle over human lives and sully them.

Carrion

AU DETOUR D'UN SENTIER, AT A TURN IN THE PATH, sometimes, we collide with a stench, as resounding as it is powerful, wall-like, fanned by the elytra of thousands of insects that make death their trade, their music and their means. We are then drawn into the poem. Baudelaire's, of course. The dark poem of life and its ending. In the open air, far from any burial place. The beauty of the sky is there, that of the lush trees, of flowers growing over bright hedges. There is the green, combed grass, the red earth, a thousand singing creatures, and then all at once you are confronted with death. Heady. Sweet. Bestial. Foul. But, ultimately, perhaps not as foul as all that. Spoiled rather, like a stew that had gone off, a bit of venison left at the bottom of a saucepan. Often, you have to put up with the stench. The remains of the creature cannot be found. Is it its ghost that smells, or our own fear? I search like this for many a corpse whose scent I have caught by chance during a game of cops and robbers in the woods of Serres,

Flainval or Hudiviller. But who is stealing what? Death has made its mark, sweeping away the spirits of a fox pierced by a local's buckshot, of an apologetic cat that has crept to die far from its owners, of a sick deer attacked by marauding dogs. And then, heat and corruption start to do their work. Swollen corpses, gases, oozing fluids. We know what happens next. An unbearably intense flower, carrion is discreet, as if it dare not show itself. Hidden. Haunted. Shy. All that remains of it is a pungent memory. Carrion becomes something that no longer exists. That no longer has any shape. The shame of life has taken refuge in foul stench. Its final residence. And then, a gust of chill wind from the Vosges, a little rain, and it's over. We pass by the same place later on and it's lily-of-the-valley that greets us, or hawthorn, while in the background a weasel slips distrustfully over the moss.

Stubble

SOMETIMES YOU IMAGINE YOU ARE LOOKING AT large skulls with close-cropped hair. Blond spikes on dry skin. A military brush-cut. It happens in late July, when it's very hot. They are harvesting. They don't thresh by hand anymore. Everything is done by machine. An enormous one, that takes up both sides of the road it travels along, and at night, in the fields, it beams lights like those of an extraterrestrial space-ship on the fields of wheat it threshes. When it is all over, what was once billowing ears of wheat is nothing but a land that has been raked over, shorn of its opulent growth. Flayed. Amputated fields. Fields fit to be ripped apart in a few weeks' time by the ploughshares and to wait in shambles for winter sowing. For the time being, the roots of the severed stalks still thrust up pointlessly into the fresh air. Strands of hard straw and grain fallen from the scoop are hidden in the furrows, reminding one of what used to be there. You walk along the Chemin des Trois Vierges and just before you arrive at the little chapel of Notre-Dame-de-Pitié, already aware of the shade of its chestnut trees and the gurgling of its spring, you pass alongside a stubble field that smells of the bakery and warm bread. Yellow eddies gust up into the sky above the remaining stubble which, depending on the curving lines of light, takes on tints of silver in places. Thick clouds. Small cyclones that wreak no havoc. You would think you were in a scene from the Bible. Indeed we are always searching for God. Birds swoop down, like a dry shower of large black drops, while the acacias look on, lined up in thorny patches along the lane. The birds strip the dying field of its last grains of fallen wheat. The sun bakes it all: the dust, the stubble, the fissured earth, the surviving lonely ears of wheat that have curiously been spared and still lie there, vulnerable and at the mercy of beaks and rodents' teeth. Dough. Yeast. Kneading. Flour and white apron. I close my eyes and I see myself pushing open the door of Rose's or Fleurantin's, the two baker's shops in rue Mathieu. I am slicing my way through the last of the cold night air on my bicycle, passing other lights speeding along to the musical hum of dynamos. Outside the bakery, my fingers numb, I push open the door as soon as it is five o'clock. The first oven wafts out its smell of warm dough, and the baguettes – we call them *flûtes* – or *bâtards*, known here as *pains longs*, are waiting lined up on the shelves or already squeezed into the wicker baskets of the first customers. They are workers from Solvay's on their way home after their night shifts, elderly folk who are unable to sleep any longer because they are too lonely, fishermen off for their early morning catch, passing lorry drivers. I slip the loaf between my coat and my thick sweater, pull up my collar, and speed off. The house has not yet woken up. I shall surprise them with the fresh bread. Crickets and larks, in unison or in opposition, do their best to carve up the daylight. I have passed the stubble fields. Their gouged surface shimmers in the heat haze. Leaning against the stone wall that extends from the chapel, I savour the shade as though it were a cool drink. Everything about yesterday and this moment is jumbled together. Feeling happy, I pedal home, for *café au lait*, butter and strawberry jam, feeling a delicious burning sensation against me, as though a sliver of sunshine had been slipped beneath my clothes.

Cabbage

LOUIS-FERDINAND CÉLINE, I BELIEVE, DESCRIBES IT
as the odour of overcooked poverty. At every meal it's a part
of the soup, without meat to enhance it, and its smell of
unwashed bodies clings to the goitrous walls of stairwells,
to outbuildings and lofts, to the low ceilings of maids' rooms,
to musty concierges' lodgings, eventually penetrating every
crack and crevice like the most ineffective of fillers. A sort of
identity card of wretchedness. Tell me what you eat, and I will
tell you what you will never be. As a child, my embarrassment
at the smell of cabbage was only equalled by my pleasure
at eating it. I would stuff my belly with it. Yes. Cabbage
soup. Hotpot. Rabbit with cabbage. Cabbage with bacon,
little Brussels sprouts, sautéed in a pan, still almost raw in
the middle, eaten on their own or with potatoes, simmered
over time in a casserole and sticking slightly to the bottom in a
thick caramel that brings all their fragrances together. My hair
and my clothing give me away in the afternoon, just as the

fillets of fried whiting do on a Friday. But on that day, we all smell of fish, and the teacher does too. Where cabbage is concerned, I am often on my own, and people hold their noses ostentatiously as I walk by. Cold cabbage is the most deadly. Something of it always lingers. Traces of the crime. Inert hazes. It's a clumsy murderer who doesn't think of concealing the evidence. It is also the smell of certain elderly people no-one loves or visits anymore. The smell of the condemned. One that hovers around old peoples' homes and remand centres. As though the cabbage were at home in large enclosed spaces, and only fit to accompany hardship and prolonged sentences, the end of life, destroyed lives, lives that are supervised, stifled, wasted, ground down – and moribund too. Cabbage is part of the sanction. And even when it's not there and never has been, you can sometimes smell it all the same, reluctantly, in rooms that are never aired, on dirty socks, upon greyish skin, under armpits, skirts or underpants, bandages. It's tenacious even when it's not there. And so commonplace, by and large, that other odours manage to mimic it and usurp its identity. In the end, it's nothing special, and that is probably why it has long been the meal of those who never were anyone, and why it always clings to them. An outcast. A reprobate. An exile. A weakling. Someone who goes unnoticed. I hope to reek of cabbage for a long time yet.

Cigar

IT IS REDOLENT OF NIGHT AND THE TROPICS. A night as thick as baker's yeast, and warm too; indeed more than warm, all-enveloping: night has become a cloak. A body. It envelops the footloose man who roams the wakeful city. Havana, Trinidad, Santiago de Cuba. Cities of the night, nights of flesh and blood, spattered with music. Everywhere. It comes, goes, engulfs, magnetises, invites, caresses. Music, and dance, its poor relation, which bring bodies together in even the most insignificant of bars, on the poorest of squares. They drink mojitos as they toss back their heads. They look for stars in the sky, but the stars are there, beside us, in eyes, upon lips, on the black shoulders glowing with sweat, the listless voices, the thighs on which dresses cleave and glisten. I wander the streets intoxicating myself on chance encounters, standing drinking in noisy green and blue bars, or sitting on the steps of locked-up, whitewashed churches. The Cuban night smells of rum, sweat and cigars, the embers of ovens improvised from motor-oil barrels in which make-do pizzas lacking tomatoes or olives are cooking. Some girls pass by, laughing a little too loudly, and the crazy fumes pursue them, chasing them with their scent of toasted cocoa beans, warm chocolate, damp leaves gnawed at by flames, age-old alcohol tended lovingly in old casks. Cigars. Like lanterns of the night, passing beacons for sailors without ships, releasing their oblong bodies – at once firm and supple, warm and cool, verdant, alive, deadly – to those who hold them in their grasping fingers and to the lips that suck them. Drink, dance, smoke, and drink some more, and dance again, and smoke the incandescent heat of a burning forest until morning, shut yourself away in the paradise of clouds that sometimes have a fragrance of leather and fur, women or wolves, earth and toast, and then, when the light of dawn dilutes the gloom of night, like a drop of liquorice in a glass of milk, set off for the sea that beats against the quaysides. Breathe it in with your eyes closed, exhausted, arms wide apart, listening to your pulse beating against the seawalls and laugh to the early morning laughter of bare-chested children rushing off to catch fish.

Cemetery

ON THE FAR SIDE OF THE ROAD, OPPOSITE OUR HOUSE, extends the domain of the dead. They lie beneath slabs of marble or granite, and pale limestone turned grey by time and weather, or inside some chapels in the case of the richest among them, but whose savings have not rescued them from the final journey. A peaceful, recumbent and flower-filled neighbourhood. A town in miniature with its impoverished, ravaged, subsiding or demolished districts, or others that are opulent, well-maintained, almost spruce, and its two or three elegant avenues where the gravel holds more firmly underfoot. Beneath are the dead, young or old, their remains disassembled or recently dug-up in earth that will take time to recover, beneath wreaths of flowers that will only outlive the deceased by a few days and will then begin to rot too. And it is this particular stench of slightly sour vegetal decomposition that still comes back to me, of stagnant water turning murky and yellowish in the glass or stone vases, those heaps of withered dahlias, those piles of faded chrysanthemums, begonias, gladioli, tired marigolds, carnations and lilies with stinking stems and covered with a tepid stickiness, deprived of their bright, pure colours like brides deserted after their wedding days by fickle young husbands, and now indistinguishable against a dull monochrome of faded beige, their distinctive characteristics vanished. A rotting heap. That is how their final resting place is described, when families have reluctantly removed the flowers from the gravestones, disappointed by how untidy they have become, and, without a qualm, have tossed them into the square of concrete that has become their own pit, and in which, like any other dying thing, they retain for a time their shape, the form of the composite wreath that once brought them together. But sometimes, too, far from these cloying odours of vegetative decay that bring an unpleasantly sugary bile to the back of my throat, there rises up a delicate fragrance of warm rock, when, on the granite of the old moss-scattered tombs, a tiny film of water that has been subjected to the glaring sun emits the scent of a forest spring, and I only have to close my eyes for the cemetery to disappear beneath the boughs of a celestial wood in which the dead have become odourless ghosts and their bodies, incorruptible beams of light.

Barber

PÈRE HENS' SALON IS ON THE CORNER OF RUE Jeanne d'Arc and chemin des Prisonniers. To get there, I simply have to take rue Saint Don and follow it as far as the crossroads. I go on my own and, as soon as I arrive, I give the barber the warm five-franc coin that I have been clasping tightly in the palm of my hand for fear that I should lose it on the way. I sit down on one of the four chairs, awaiting my turn. Père Hens smokes and prances about as he trims. He's an ageless man, dressed in a grey nylon smock, small, slim, with brushed-back silvery hair that he frequently combs, his eyes constantly creased by the smoke of the Gauloise that never leaves the right-hand corner of his lips. He circles around his customer, bouncing about with the gracefulness of a boxer whose strong point is his footwork. He talks a great deal, to men of course. That's all there are. Old men mostly. He doesn't seem to see me until it's my go: "Your turn, lad!" He makes me sit down on the revolving chair, raises it to its maximum height by activating it with his foot, as though he were blowing up an inflatable mattress with a hydraulic pump. With the flamboyant action of a toreador or a magician, he swirls a flimsy cape around me and, apart from my head and my neck, I disappear under it. Putting a finishing touch to the preparations, he pulls from a large roll on the dressing-table a length of white crêpe paper edged with pink and wraps this elastic collar, which is both soft yet rough and tickles my chin pleasantly, around my neck. For half an hour, I am left to the mercy of his scissors, which he likes to make chatter and sing as he snips the air here and there as though, at the same time as me, he were cutting the transparent locks of tousle-haired ghosts. The smoke from the hand-rolled and ready-made cigarettes of the customers, thick and acrid, forms a moving ceiling that shifts as he hops around. I like being left to his mercy, just as nowadays I still like being left in the hands of often wonderfully talkative female hairdressers, masseuses, osteopaths, chiropodists and physiotherapists. As my light brown hair falls around me, my bird-like skull is revealed. The best moment is still to come. The haircut over, Père Hens tears off the crêpe paper that has disguised me as one of Charles IX's courtiers, rubs it between his hands, tosses it into the dustbin and picks up a bulbous metal flask, with a long slender spout, at the other end of which hangs a large pear of slightly cracked red rubber. Then, still very lively, he skips around me as he squeezes the pear and sprays a cloud of cold water that smells of roses and brilliantine and also, a little, of his old dog. This microscopic rain deposits its refreshing shower in tiny droplets over my close-cropped hair, my eyebrows, my forehead, my closed mouth and my neck. A secular monthly baptism. You smell nice. You look lovely, my mother says to me when I get back home. I believe her. It's an age when we always believe what our mothers tell us.

Suntan lotion

MY MOTHER MISTRUSTS THE SUN AS THOUGH IT were a hostile enemy that never lowers its guard. I've been brought up in this constant fear that a body, if overheated, runs the risk of agonising pain if it is brusquely plunged into cold water. A fear of burns, too, of injuries to the skin that risk damaging it irreversibly. I have to wait until mid-afternoon before going to join my friends at the swimming pool. Actually, it's a simple bathing area with fresh, peaty-brown, running water – rather slow-running, in fact – that is none other than that of the River Meurthe. A few decades earlier, on one of its tributaries, upstream from the weir, some concrete partitions were put in place to create pools. On the bank, there is a row of solid-looking cabins in which you can get changed. There is a till where you buy your ticket, some lifeguards, and also perhaps – I am no longer certain – a refreshment bar. Large trees, poplars and ashes, the tops of which rustle as they stroke the sky, shade the entire area. I am itching to go since it's already late. My mother has forced me to have an unbearable siesta during which I didn't sleep a wink. Outside, it's mid-July, there's a hum of grasshoppers and crickets, and the holidays stretch on endlessly. I've slipped on my swimming costume, which she has pulled up to my navel and which accentuates my thinness. I've put on my plastic sandals. From an orange aerosol canister, she squirts out a large white dollop that has the consistency of shaving foam. She sprays this dollop onto my skin. It's smooth. She rubs it in and it soon becomes invisible, miraculously dissolving all over my body. I read the label on the bottle. Ambre solaire. It sounds like the title of one of those poems I learn every week, written by Emile Verhaeren, Maurice Fombeure, José-María de Heredia, Paul-Jean Toulet. I close my eyes. I breathe in. A rather greasy substance, faintly musky, a scent of Turkish gynoecium. Like an extension of the heat of the day, the warmth of intimacy, a caressing arm. Later on, I shall discover the elderly Ingres' Turkish bathers. I shall associate this smell with them. I am ready at last. I get on my bike. I set off. I sniff the wind. I'm ten years old. The present is a wonderful gift.

Two-stroke

YOUTH CAN SOMETIMES BE MERELY A MATTER OF noise and of smoke, not always of anger. In the early 1970s, the important thing was to be able to backfire or put-put and make sure everyone heard it. Blue or grey *mobylettes* with filed-off carburettors and stripped-down exhaust-pipes, souped-up by whatever means available, and handlebars so close together that they could almost be held in one hand, making every bend perilous. A two-seat saddle, a fox's tail over the back mudguard, a rear-view mirror adorned with a curly mount. A short stand so that you could tilt the beast backwards in the Harley way. The best of them have the basic features of the Gitane Testi, the Flandria and the Malaguti, fiendish miniature machines with a cubic capacity, however, not exceeding 50 cm^3 and tanks that are filled with a two-stroke mixture, half-petrol, half-oil, a generous dual type which, when combusted, gives off a smell of overheated frying. We love the dances, or rather the local *baloches* where the orchestras with their sequins and sideburns reverberate every Saturday night in a rectangular caravan that carries the standard tunes of the French demi-gods of rock-and-roll to small towns and villages, as well as the glittering shows of Drupi or Mike Brant, that conquer girls' hearts as well as their arms. "Vado via", "Laisse-moi t'aimer", "Qui saura?" We watch this from afar, still lost in our milk-tooth innocence. The dance comes together before our eyes, and already the circle of tuned-up bikes is creating its racetrack haze and din. Twenty-year-old boys wear shoulder-length hair, cut in the style of the Rubettes or, at best, that of Bowie of the Ziggy Stardust period or Keith Richards at the time of "Exile on Main Street". Short imitation leather jackets, tight-fitting Shetland sweaters that stop above the navel, bell-bottom trousers held up by a belt with a large buckle, dark red shoes with rounded ends and high heels. Molière boots, as they were called. Girls in miniskirts or Karting pants climb on to small motorbikes, giving a glimpse of their thighs. They wear boots, satin blouses with high collars, green eyeshadow and eyelashes laden with mascara. They smoke Fine 120 or Royale Menthol Extra-longues and their lovers smoke Gauloises. In the newspapers the following day we read that rival gangs have clashed, using flick-knives, axes or bicycle chains, outside the dance hall or even inside it. We hang around the area trying to spot traces of blood on the ground. All we do is breathe in the stale stench of beer, urine and vomit. On summer evenings, these machines pass to and fro in front of our house, along the road to Sommerviller, creating clouds of smoke and a piercing din, challenging each other to foolish dares that cause more than one of them to crash into an innocent plane tree or beneath the wheels of a truck. Inhaling the warm smell of these pulsating engines, I think I can catch a whiff of adult life just as when, in the first flickers of dawn, you try to gauge what kind of weather it will be later in the day. I am eager to ride one of these machines and smell its garage stench and feel the wind in my hair. Dombasle still, to this day, retains this tradition of flimsy, small-cylinder bikes that scream and emit their blue burned-oil smoke as they hurl themselves around bends, knees brushing the ground, Grand Prix style. The scooters ridden by the sons have replaced the little mopeds belonging to the fathers, who, from their days of glory and punch-ups, still have a few scars from knife wounds, some doe-eyed girls tattooed beneath their cheek-bones, three fewer teeth, a silver bracelet and some improbable boots. Their once bare, flat bellies sag beneath their tracksuit tops. They mow their narrow patches of lawn behind their houses. Occasionally, they kneel down to adjust their motors which splutter and consume a little too much, then, with their soldering iron, they light their barbecue so as to grill defrosted sausages while they drink a beer or two bought at the discount store. An overweight wife joins them on the bench. She often wears the same type of tracksuit as they do. Once upon a time she looked like Joëlle, the pretty lead singer of the Il était une fois band who died at the age of twenty-seven. The dances disappeared a long time ago, but they still listen to Johnny Hallyday. Sometimes, on Sundays, as they wander around a village car-boot sale, where they go because they've got to do something, they come across a Gitane Testi, lying on the pavement between two boxes of old vinyl records and military jackets. They stop and look at it. It seems very small to them. They would have imagined it much bigger. Like life.

Communal showers

AS FAR AS FOOTBALL IS CONCERNED, MY ONLY memories are mucky and cold. Mud-spattered. Unpleasant. Long Wednesdays spent training under coal-black skies, unrelenting rain, deafened by the noise and sooty fumes of the trains that pass by not far from the stadium – red and cream-coloured railcars emitting gas-oil smoke – as well as the barking of our trainer, a short, stocky man who fantasises to us about Gerd Müller, Paul Breitner, Kevin Keegan, Johann Cruyff, Dominique Bathenay. The matches take place on Saturdays, but I never take part in them. I stay on the bench on the touchline, only belonging to the team in as much as I am the substitute, ready to bound onto the pitch like a large cat, fully believing the lies of the trainer who tells me: "Claudel, I'm keeping you in reserve, you're my last trump card!" My friends run around, shouting, hoping, kicking the ball, scoring goals, hugging one another. I am cut off from it all. Forgotten. Ignored. The last trump card is never used. I'm deprived of the fun. I pack my immaculate kit into my bag. My mother won't have to wash it. She'll be the happy one. I comfort myself by collecting the Panini pictures of our idols. They come as stickers and smell of plastic. For two seasons I never miss a single training session. I throw myself into it wholeheartedly. I obey all instructions. I want to shine, to be noticed by the trainer, so as to be on the match team-sheet when it is put up in the window of the café Le Globe on Friday evening for the following Saturday. Occasionally, the trainer favours me with a comment, "You've amazed me again, Claudel!", which I take as encouragement, whereas, in actual fact, he is making fun of my incompetence, which has led me to score an own-goal yet again. October, November, December, January, February, March: the pitch becomes boggy and we push the ball around like convicts moving wheelbarrows full of stones. At the end of the session, we look like barbarian gods, covered in wet and mud. The changing rooms are unheated. The studs echo on the floor. We take off our heavy kit that has become brown all over. Our breath comes in short puffs of mist. There's a smell of animal fat, camphor, menthol, arnica and wormwood. We all use Baume du Castor to warm our thigh muscles before playing. You can't hear what anyone's saying. Cries, laughter, jostling, merry insults, feigned scuffles, belches, farts, jeers. Everyone's stark naked. I make my way towards the showers, both hands shielding a barely formed penis, a ridiculously thin and timid snail-like thing, hairless and ashamed, whereas others, like the Voiry boy who's very proud of his, are already showing off their competitive cocks – long as bananas, hairy, arrogant, mocking – holding them in their hands, showing them to everybody, whirling them around. Boiling water spurts out of rusty nozzles. The walls are made of concrete, the floor of cement. We disappear in the steam of a Turkish bath. We all have the same Palmolive soap. The foam streams between our feet. All at once it's hot, but despite the clean fragrances the old background smell, which is the real hallmark of the place, still lingers, a fusty stench of dampness and tiled walls, of unhealthy old buildings, the pointing ravaged by mould, and sugary condensation. I hide my little willy as best I can. As I soap myself, I am dreaming of next Saturday. The trainer sends me onto the pitch. Only ten minutes remain. We are 6–0 down. I run around in every direction, distributing the ball. I make incisive passes. Impossible headers. Return volleys just like Jean-Michel Larqué. We are catching up thanks to me. I can't stop scoring. Everyone in the stadium is shouting my name: "Claudel! Claudel!" They carry me in triumph after the final whistle has blown. The last trump has finally struck. I, too, will soon have my photo on a Panini sticker.

Clean sheets

IT'S ON SUNDAY EVENINGS THAT MY MOTHER PUTS clean sheets on the beds, sheets in which she has trapped the day's breeze. Most of all I like these fresh sheets in wintertime, when the north wind has beaten them and stiffened them – sometimes frozen them – and they retain something snowy and glacial from their lashing, the grainy white flesh of their ancient cloth becomes even rougher. Sleeping on my own is something I have never enjoyed. Even as a child I miss another body. Its heat, its strength, its softness, its warm breath and the beating of its heart. Falling asleep often makes me fear the worst, which is not death, but being left alone, endless solitude. The very next day, I have to go back to boarding school and its vast dormitory, with its shiny floor, its cheap wooden cupboards, its narrow beds. One of the two men in charge is called Fiacre. He terrifies me. It's said that he's a former soldier. Apparently, he's also a music lover and plays the violin. Sometimes, when he's drunk, he hits me, as well as the others, for no reason. Every evening I cry silently, hiding my tears from my friends as well as the other supervisors, Monsieur Fix and Monsieur Bossu. I feel desperate in this place that oozes inhuman tedium. But on Sunday evenings, in between my fresh sheets, sleep is delicious, for I snuggle into the night with that smell of the great outdoors within me. It has permeated the crisp material in the fresh air throughout the day, and when I lay my face on the sheet and have turned off the bedside light, I seem to be inhaling the vastnesses of Prussia, Russia, Manchuria, Mongolia and Siberia, all stitched together and captured for my own selfish happiness. It's not just a scent of washed, clean linen that I imbibe, but a geography of earth and wind, broad and wild, distilled from an endless number of stories, fables, songs and images that I have read and seen, and that have made of me – at home, on the point of falling asleep, in this bed that's covered with its new sheets that my grandmothers' and great-aunts' patient needles once adorned with flowers, curves and arabesques – a celestial and tranquil traveller, a vulnerable creature who knows that for the time being he is swathed and happy.

Ironmonger

LET US ISSUE THE FINAL ROLL-CALL FOR THE SMALL shop: the ironmonger, the haberdashery, the saddler, the fruit-monger, the *triperie*, the horse butcher, the grocery store, the seed merchant, the dairy, the milliner, the general store, the hosier, the cobbler, the hardware shop. Time is closing their doors and taking down the signs without posting official notices anywhere. We therefore forget to send our condolences. And in any case, to whom should we send them? There are few tears, few regrets. On the contrary, we seem delighted by the concentration of so many varied worlds in one noisy place. A notable oddity in our nomadic age: I still live in the place where I was born. The size of the town hasn't changed. The only things that thrive here, in the deserted areas, are hairdressing salons and local branches of banks. I know, however, that behind the façades there are ghost-like shops that continue to sell to a diminishing clientele, whose discretion is matched only by their invisibility, pearl buttons, string, hempseed, leather straps, cord by the metre, bundles of raffia, nails by the bushel, horse-meat sausages, medlars, tripe and offal. The noises from the street stop as soon as you push open certain doors. A shrill bell drips out its discordant notes. Someone is looking us up and down from beneath heavy spectacles. The ironmonger in his white overall, wearing a severe and worried expression, whose relationship with the great chemists of long ago is clear to me. The name of the shop, the *droguerie*, and that of its tenant, take me far back, to a distant time when chemists were still called apothecaries. The ironmonger's shop is a relic; the ironmonger is from another age. It is the place of cleanliness par excellence, where you can find everything to clean anything that can get dirty: skin, wood, iron, copper, brass, tiles, windows; or anything that can become blocked: pipes, drains, lavatories. Powders, paints, solvents, dissolvents, paint-strippers, hard or liquid soaps, poisons, fertiliser, rat bait, nitrates, sulphates, chlorates, caustic soda, quicklime, varnishes, sealants, bitumens, fillers, nothing here is edible, except for those desperate gamblers who would like to throw it all in. Many tins or bottles have skull and crossbones on them. The ironmonger lives dangerously, and the customer too. From this quiet laboratory, chaos, explosions, poisoning, sudden and certain death on a mass scale, as well as murder, can result. And yet the shelves look peaceful enough. Order prevails, and gravity too. The butcher is entitled to make jokes, the dairyman may be bawdy, the fishmonger may talk in a loud voice and whistle a popular tune. Whereas the ironmonger handles his language as he does his products.

He doesn't raise his voice. He doesn't use rough words. He is ready to give evidence in court. The place is a church of another kind, laboratory-like and stringent, where the nostrils burn on contact with the miasmas of detergents and are overwhelmed and seduced by the glues and varnishes. The greasy mastics smell of butter, ammonia, under-washed genitals; the liquid soaps, as smooth as streams of silver fir honey, belie their viscous nature by lightening it with hints of lemon. We are immersed in a daily chemistry, in the conjugated artificiality of powders and liquids, gases and solids, and a realisation that everything has an alternative aspect, something worrying, metallic, inhuman, cold-bloodedly technical, and possibly lethal.

Church

WE ALWAYS TRY TO CREATE KEYS EVEN WHEN THERE
are no locks. I have always loved churches. I used to visit them
a great deal, when I believed in God, and I still do today, when
I no longer believe. I like the curious etiquette of their silence.
Their withdrawal from the world too, even in the heart of the
noisiest cities. Their walls take you out of yourself, out of time,
away from the madness of objects and human beings. I'm a
child again, a choirboy, stirred by the beauty of the "theatre
of the Mass", as Jean Giono described it, inhaling the warm
wax that falls in slow tears down the sides of the large candles
in the silver branches of the candelabra, and the fumes of
incense, acrid, thick, spiralling upwards as they escape from
the thurible like the visible soul of some sacrificed Satan, but
becalmed later when they rise in a timorous haze to defy
the impassivity of the stained-glass windows. Albs, cassocks,
stoles, scapulars, lacework, belts made of satin or rough cord.
The starched vestments are stored in a tall cupboard in the

sacristy, shining with polish and smelling of eau de cologne and lavender. The fabrics are impregnated with the fragrance. We put them on in silence beneath the pious gaze of a thin-lipped, churchy woman who is our sergeant-major: Mother Julia. Candle, polish, incense, demure materials woven by devoted hands, stone tiles washed in plenty of water by women on their knees, between two "Our Fathers", the priest's winey breath after the Eucharist and, above all, the faith of millions of human beings over the centuries who exude that very particular smell that is one of dogged, profound and enduring piety. The odour of unshakeable belief in a marvellous illusion that has lasted for two thousand years, and which has sustained many, and killed many others.

Sleeping child

NOTHING CAN REVEAL MORE ABOUT WHO WE ARE or what we once were, than the fragrance of the skin of a sleeping child, snug in its bed, mouth half-open, without the least fear or dread, for the child knows that we are all there, close and ready to ward off the darkness, dissolve it or deny it if need be. When my daughter was very young, I would occasionally go into her bedroom at night because I thought I could hear her groaning, or crying perhaps, and the notion that she could be suffering, even in a dream, was so unbearable to me that I would wake from my unsettled fatherly sleep and go to her. She is still asleep on her back, her arms in the air, on either side of her face, little hands outstretched, fingers open, her plump cheeks, and her long eyelashes closed like exquisite and delicate blinds over her beautiful, invisible eyes. I stay there for a long time, gazing at her as one gazes at a marvel without really believing it, without actually believing that she is real and bound to us by ties that nothing can ever loosen, not even death, despite all its powers. In the half-light, I can see her little chest rising, softly, and falling, still softly, and rising again, and I can't pull myself away from this motion, that is the manifestation of life, its hopes and its fragility. I lay a finger on her hands. I brush her cheeks , her forehead, her fine black hair, silky and warm, and, without a sound, I lean over to kiss her neck. It's as if I were discovering the naked sleeping child, pressed to its equally naked mother, in Gustav Klimt's very beautiful painting, "The Three Ages of Women", which depicts a moment of everyday intimacy, of a noble and prolific humanity, a painting showing the sweet warmth of flesh and perspiration, of trust in the soundest of sleeps, when nothing can happen to us. It is like a dazzling plunge into the most natural of fragrances, that of life at its very earliest stage, when it is merely softness, nourished with caresses and milk, smiles and nursery rhymes, by hands that guard, reassure and protect. The fragrance of the very first moments, of tender flesh, of creams and talcum powder. The fragrance of that sheltered childhood, gentle and babbling, calm, serene, and which, regrettably, slips away from us all too quickly, as we set out on the road, standing gradually taller, walking alone, with nothing remaining ultimately of what we once were, frail creatures cradled in trusting surrender within the arms and smiles of those who created us.

Stable

WE LIVE ALONGSIDE ANIMALS: RABBITS, HENS, ducks, cats, dogs, geese, turkeys too, in household gardens, in courtyards, in kitchens that welcome chicks and ducklings into their warmth. And further away, but very nearby all the same, cows, pigs, horses, sheep and ewes, goats, donkeys, mules, hinnies, bulls and oxen, in the fields and the farms. Close by is the Poulets' farm, on rue Mathieu. And then the others, not much further away, those belonging to the Guillaumonts, the Roussels, the Dehans, in the small town, within its actual boundaries, and a part of it. The streets are spattered at times with dung and cowpats, which we rush to collect to throw on the roots of hydrangeas or rose bushes. The herds go by. An impressive and unforgettable sight. In the surrounding villages, Sommerviller, Flainval, Bauzemont, Crévic, Maixe, Haraucourt, the animals are at peace. The unfenced forecourt known as the *usoir* still accumulates large piles of manure. Wealth is gauged in this way, by the amount discarded. The smell of straw and excrement mingled together is an indication of affluence and riches. Men and animals together. Feeding one another. Knowing one another. The milk drunk comes from udders you can see, smell, touch. Stable doors for me are like those of churches: they open onto a mystery and a silence barely disrupted by exhalations or slow movements, by warm breath, by both the poetry of incense and the chewing of the cud. A moment of contemplation. In the darkness the Eucharist is being celebrated. The scent of a manger, of course, in which the tart smell of the newborn child is sweetened by the breath of the ass and the gentle ox. In the depths of the stable, all you can see are the cattle's rear ends, their tails swinging to a gentle rhythm, their long backs stretched over their vertebrae and their heavy flanks like boats at anchor. Occasionally they stir, emitting a warmth that has a whiff of digestion, of curdled milk, of dung and chewed hay, a good smell fermented with life and weariness, inactivity and milking, muddy hides and saliva. The flies are drawn in, irritating and audacious, buzzing around the animals, driven crazy by their sweat, then they glue themselves to the ceiling, temporarily confounded. A cat wanders in, mewing, and with its delicate pink tongue laps a little milk from a cavity in the hardened ground. The scene and the smells that one contemplates and inhales are a thousand years old. As though mankind had come to a standstill. Closing our eyes, we become once more the ancient peoples of Mesopotamia, the Nile, or Attica.

Ether

IT'S WHAT WE USE TO KILL KITTENS AND TO HELP children sleep. Its modest name conceals a heartless hypocrite, its heavenly poetry a murderer. I am five years old. I am holding my mother's hand and we are walking along the corridors of the main hospital in Nancy. We pass nurses and sisters wearing coifs. Sometimes, an open door onto a ward reveals prone bodies some of whose bandaged members rise up in curious contortions. Groans. The stench of ointment and rotten skin. A woman on her knees is mopping the beige and black tiles with a cloth. Bleach. I shall see her again many years later, imprisoned in a painting by Cézanne. We avoid her as we would if we were playing hopscotch. They show us into a room. Two beds next to one another. I shall sleep beside my mother. Happiness. Towards evening, men in white coats come in, one is older and taller, with a pear-shaped face – Louis XIV among his deferential court. He palpates my throat, makes me open my mouth, stick my tongue out, and addresses himself in complicated words to his subjects who surround him, heads bowed. I am sitting on the edge of the bed, my feet hanging freely. He taps my cheek and tells me I won't feel a thing. In the morning, I am not allowed any breakfast. They take me away from my mother. I glide down long corridors on a trolley, with my eyes on the ceiling. All of a sudden, it feels cold, there are merciless round lights, as blinding as Arctic sunlight, and people with masked faces, dressed in white and wearing caps, are bustling around strange apparatus and preparing steel instruments. I recognise the voice of Louis XIV who, once again, tells me that I won't feel a thing, and that I'm a big boy. A double lie. Another liar comes over, holding an iron mask. He tells me that I'm going to fall asleep peacefully. I don't want to go to sleep. A new traitor joins him and holds me still. The iron mask covers my face and withdraws me from the world. A nauseating stench of rubber invades my mouth and my nostrils, followed very quickly by my discovery of the existence of the violently chemical and glacial fumes of ether. I become kitten-like. They want to take me away from the litter. I struggle. I call for my mother. My tearful voice rebounds against the walls of the mask. There's a revulsion, an emptiness, and darkness. Ever since then, I know that death smells of ether. And I continually prepare for that final loss of breath.

Campfire

WE HAVE SET OFF IN TEAMS, WE WEAR UNIFORMS and every morning we hoist the flag. Shorts that are always too large, pale blue short-sleeved shirts, black scarves tied in a neckerchief and that vary according to age. Our dormitories are former barracks which, for a number of years, accommodated the surviving inhabitants of the village of Martincourt, whose houses had been destroyed by the Germans. In the mornings, we devote ourselves to activities such as pottery, glazing, weaving, making comets, wood carving, modelling, potato printing, macramé. At lunchtime, we eat chips that are too greasy, pasta that is overcooked, steaks that are too hard, beans that have been boiled for too long. The siesta is compulsory. We pretend we are asleep. Our supervisors whisper in the corridors. Then it's time for the walk, in Indian file or in pairs, a handkerchief knotted at each corner by way of headgear, and a tin flask hanging from our belts. We walk for ages. We have our afternoon snack beside a path, among poppies or cornflowers, in a clearing, by a stream, or in the shade of tall lime trees on a village square. We eat bread and jam, stewed fruit, Vache qui rit cheese, and hard, lumpy chocolate, in slim bars, that has a bitter taste. We shoo away the wasps and drink mint or liquorice cordial. Twice a week, a huge game is organised. The teams are given names of animals: the Beavers, the Otters, the Bears, the Wolves, the Foxes. We track down clues in the Saint-Jean woods, near the ford on the Esch, find banners, and answer riddles. There are evening activities. One supervisor plays the guitar, another the harmonica. We sing "Jolie bouteille, sacrée bouteille", "Santiano", "Donne du rhum à ton homme". Some come up with sketches that make fun of the man in charge or the matron. Others clown around, perform magic tricks or tell scary stories. We sing one last song, "Vent frais, vent du matin", to soothe us, and we return in silence to our dormitory. Lights dimmed. Everyone to bed. Night-time. I can cry at last. For these summer camps that last an entire month, and which I've been on every year from the age of four to thirteen, make me unhappy, just as my first years at boarding school would make me unhappy later on. Time hangs heavily. It's an unshakeable lump of lead. I miss my mother so. I can't understand why she sends me away like this. I have actually never understood and I've never dared to ask her. But, midst this calamity and this punishment, there is nevertheless one great miracle: the campfire. We prepare the fire throughout our stay. It grows like a faceless clock marking time. We build it up very carefully, using all the wood at our disposal, discarded planks, dried branches of wild broom, old rags, pallets, dead wood gathered from the forest, worm-eaten beams donated by country folk, broken-up crates. As the days go by, the structure rises to the sky. It becomes a composite tower of Babel and we follow its gradual construction eagerly. When the long-awaited evening finally arrives, we are both excited and solemn. We eat in silence and then, in an almost formal way, we make our way in teams to the pyre and take our places around it, sitting cross-legged on the grass which the falling dusk has already "dressed with pearls of dew" as André Hardellet might have written. We wait a bit longer, so that the twilight in the west doesn't spoil the moment, and when darkness has settled, a supervisor lights a torch made of pitch and cloth. When it's ablaze with flames, he tosses it into the mound and the huge, cone-shaped mass catches fire, from its base to its crest, casting its rust and lemon-coloured flames up into the dark sky. I could spend hours in front of this enormous fire, letting it warm and engulf me as it impregnates my skin, my clothes and my hair with its crackling smell of charred wood, watching it as it collapses and shoots forth clusters of sparks – red, gold and pale yellow – leaping and flickering, and creating an apocalyptic glimmer such as I would discover later in the paintings of Monsù Desiderio. To me it also seems that the smell of this vast fire, with its appalling heat and its smouldering entrails, is connecting me to the wonders of the first men who hunted animals and, at night, cooked their food by it, kept the cold at bay, and sharpened the tips of their spears. In a confused way, beneath the stars towards which red particles, like burning insects, are rising upwards, I feel all at once like a member of a very ancient community. The huge fire twists and dances for me. The next day, my entire body will retain its wild scent of smoke, of snapping embers and warm ashes, and, like an animal sniffing around in quest of fresh prey, I shall breathe it in for a long time.

Hay

WE SAVOUR WHAT IS GOLDEN. FOR A SMELL MAY have a colour. And shapes too. Flattened hay, swathes, haystacks, hayricks, sheaves, parallelepipeds, large cylinders that look as though they were deposited by a secretive spaceship. Beneath the continuous sun, the damp evaporates from hour to hour. An open-air oven that cooks on a slow heat, without burning. This process is clearly visible in the shadows that Monet sculpts like wells of blackness against the crooked sides of his painted sheaves of hay. Mechanical, rotatory movements, when the metal rods of the tedding-machine whirl round on their axis, in a friendly roar, and the hay flies away, comes back, then settles once more over the ground where the crickets' nests are laid bare, along with the vole's network of burrows. Back to hand-held instruments when the land is too steep, or too narrow for a tractor to pass. The fine wooden rake with its rough teeth is brought out, light to carry. They shake out the grass which, after a day in the heat, has already changed shade, the green having given way to bronze. They comb it as though it were a great mop of hair. Skylarks flutter about, calling shrilly in the blue-tinged June air. Sometimes, you lie down right in the middle of the hay, to rest, to kiss someone you love, surrounded by the scent of passion, by the fragrances of the seed, and of the dust to which certain delicate grasses are reduced, like lysis, also known as quaking-grass, which sticks to our sweat. You stretch out and fall asleep in the vast fibrous bedding, soft and itchy, while you wait to pack it, load it and cram it to the rafters into barns and haylofts. The bodily movements of the men – my father among them, whom I see near Ménil-sur-Belvitte, in the Vosges countryside – which consist of stabbing the prongs of a fork into a sheaf and lifting it, with no apparent effort, as high as possible while extending the handle at arm's length so that the person on top of the cart, which is almost completely laden, can grab it and put it in place. Later on, in the milder months, venturing like a thief into the huge space – sometimes on two levels, and lit only by the light seeping through the tiles – of a farm hayloft. There to be gripped once more by this captive gold. Climbing to the very top of the beams, and letting yourself jump down onto the loose hay into which you sink as though plunging into a large, warm hand, while the fat neutered cat that you have disturbed bounds away. At about the age of eleven, in the dustiness that hay creates in the air of the barns and on the large decorated boards of their wooden floors, I also make a discovery. It is in the beautiful pass of Straiture, a valley that looks Tyrolean in parts, and that links Fraize to Gérardmer. A children's holiday camp that moves from place to place, we camp wherever we happen to be on our walk, asking for board and lodging from local farmers. Sleeping in the hay, between friends, with just the light, crushable grass to cover us, brimming with the scent of the soft, fresh air; hollowing out a nest in it as though we were in a clean pigsty, and disappearing, happily drowning, into its vast womb. After a few hours alas, I am on my feet in the cold night air, suffocating, beneath the lofty gaze of Betelgeuse and Vega. My lungs seem to have disappeared. I gasp for air, but I can't breathe. I'm a fish cast on the shore. I'm suffocating. I'm going to die. Without my realising, it is the first symptom of the asthma that will be with me for ever, an irksome life companion, torturous and unpredictable, but to which, after violent attacks, I nevertheless owe long, peaceful hours, bedridden, exhausted, distraught, far from other people, and thanks to which reading and writing attain a degree of pleasure, a fragile and miraculous form of coming back to life.

Manure

THE SOIL NEEDS TO BE FED IF, IN TURN, WE WANT IT to feed us. Every two years, in March, my father buys a lorry-load of manure from Robert Domgin, a local Sommerviller farmer, who comes to deliver it in person, dumping the lot on the sloping terrain that adjoins our house. The dark avalanche slips down with a smooth, silky rustling noise and comes to a halt, steaming. For a few days, our house becomes saturated with animal stenches of urine, excrement and fermented straw. This is a considerable part of what has been produced by the lower bellies of a herd wintering in the cowshed. On cold days, and on nights that are colder still, the warm pile is wreathed in languid fumes, as though an inner fire, either too feeble or concealed, were continuing its action without ever display-ing the slightest flame. I open the windows wide so that the powerful smell can spread into all the rooms. It seems to me that it's reminding me of my ancestors, most of them smallholding farmers, from Lorraine and from the Morvan.

My father is digging. I am carrying the buckets, and I am pushing the wheelbarrow over to him. The pile grows smaller. I am worn out, but I feel proud. The manure is being forked onto the open earth in which fat worms, brutally plucked from their holes, unfurl the rings of their pink bodies as they escape. My father fills in the trench again. All that can be seen of the manure now is a few stalks of rotten, yellow straw that stick out here and there like dirty hair from the furrowed ground. The coldness of the earth, its solid humidity and its heavy blackness absorb the organic matter and smother it. The various smells mingle together and cancel one another out. The fumes fade away. We are standing on top of a stomach that is in the process of digesting a substantial meal without a sound. And while I hand my father a large handkerchief with which he can mop his forehead, and while I savour this male complicity that brings us together at such moments, I would not be especially surprised to hear a solemn, subterranean belch, as if the sated telluric and coprophagous divinities were thanking us.

Gauloises and Gitanes

ONE IS EITHER GAULOISES OR GITANES. JUST as one is either Radio Télévision Luxembourg or Europe 1, Peugeot or Citroën, Pernod or Ricard. The very old smoke shag, those who are not as old smoke dark tobacco or caporal, and the others, we children, smoke dried sorb leaves, known to us as "smoking wood", which gives us dreadful diarrhoea. My Uncle Dédé smokes Gauloises. He works in the salt mine in Varengéville. People simply say the "Saltworks", and everybody understands. His job fascinates me because it is carried out underground. "Just there, actually," my uncle says to me one day, pointing, with his fingers round a lit cigarette, at the ground beneath my feet. For someone who already relishes mythology as much as I do, to come across men from your own family, from the streets and the neighbourhood, who visit the Underworld every day is enough to endow them with a sacrosanct importance. Uncle Dédé smokes like a trooper, even though he's a miner. I've always known him with a pack of Gauloises in his pocket or in his hand, with a cigarette between his lips and a deep-rooted hollow cough, and the little house he lives in at 34 rue Louis Burtin – formerly rue des Ecoles – with Aunt Jeanine, retains at night and by day the acrid and irritant whiff of dark tobacco: furniture, carpet, curtains, clothing, hair, breath, skin, everything is infused with the smell of Gauloises. I love it because I am fond of those who smell of it. As soon as my uncle and aunt have left our house after a visit and an aperitif, my mother opens the windows wide. The ashtray is full to the brim and the sitting room is clouded with a thin haze that settles in and refuses to budge. Personally, I'd like this whiff of Gauloises to remain for a long time because it mocks the smell of our house, imposing its foreign presence and recalling, too, those moments I love when "le Gros" and "la Canard" – those are my uncle's and aunt's nicknames – come to visit us, interrupting the humdrum quality of a daily life that at times I find too tame. The men of that generation are reluctant subjects for experimentation: they doggedly coat their lungs with tar, loath to relinquish the soft blue packet, decorated with the Gallic helmet, while at the same time, in their jobs, they are obliged to inhale highly toxic substances and gases, often without being warned about them. A bit like guinea pigs sent to the front line. Gitanes smokers are different to Gauloises smokers. Frequently, they do not belong to the same social class. The proletariat buy the latter. The managerial classes, service professions, foremen, teachers and engineers use the former, the tobacco of which is also brown and emits a smoke that seems harsher to me, more aggressive, less insouciant, thinner and slightly dry – in a word, almost aloof – compared to the generous bonhomie, the unrefined and pleasantly coarse reek of Gauloises. Gitanes have a hard, cardboard pack that is wide and rectangular. Gauloises have a soft upright pack. Father Thouvenin smokes Gitanes. One or two packs a day. Just like Father Bastien and Father Silvy-Leligois. The Gitane is priestly. It probably prolongs the magic of incense. I like these priests very much. Father Thouvenin, especially. I've a great deal of respect for him. He is completely immersed in his faith, but he doesn't make a big thing of it. He plays the guitar. He's young. He's slim. He's straightforward. He's poor. He smiles very little, and always sadly. I still often think of him, even though I saw him for the last time in 1975. And as I learned from a brief obituary notice in *L'Est Républicain* a few years ago, he now smokes his Gitanes right next to God.

Tar

DURING THE LONG-DRAWN-OUT HOURS OF SUMMER, along the narrow roads lined with ripe fields of wheat, the sun collides with the asphalt's crust, in amongst the grey gravel, creating black trickles of thick, shiny oil that sticks to the tyres of cars and bicycles as well as to the soles of the wanderer. It smells of pounded stone, of the dust from gunpowder, of camphorated pitch and the unexpected hint of iodine in these lands far from any sea, other than the one which, millions of years ago, covered everything around here, hollows and valleys, and left nothing behind apart from shells that have turned into heavy and brittle rocks, and which the ploughshares bring to the surface in their ghostly trawling. Long, endless afternoons between Haraucourt, Buissoncourt, Réméréville and Courbesseaux, free to roam at will. Or as a camper walking in disciplined single file along the roads of Martincourt, Gézoncourt, Mamey, Rogéville, Arnould, Corcieux, singing those ridiculous, repetitive marching songs about noodles, wooden legs and the best way of walking. The tar sweats in the heat while the grasshoppers and crickets tune their wings. Among the round, white-bellied clouds, the larks send back their response. You find yourself dreaming by a gurgling spring. You gaze at the copses in the distance, near Saint-Jean, that look like large blue sheep lying on their sides. You inhale deeply. A wasp blown off course by a brief gust of wind sometimes gets stuck in the blistering slicks of the molten road surface. It dies alone, without any attempt to extricate itself from the trap it understands is fatal. Three o'clock chimes on the bell towers of the villages shimmering in the heat-haze, and the bronze echoes fade away lethargically into the utterly indifferent sky. The tar also comes in iron barrels. It's in liquid form. It's waiting for Algerian or Portuguese workers to draw large bucketfuls from it to repair the potholes in the road. All this is stored near our primary school. We keep a watch on the contents. The colour and smell of liquorice. Bet you won't throw a large stone into it. They dare me. I take up the challenge. The frailty of idiots. The tar spatters everywhere. The barrel has lost part of its contents. The ground is smeared. Criminal behaviour. I run away. I'm certain they're going to arrest me. I arrive back at the house, looking sheepish. My mother knows something is up. The doorbell rings. I can see two kepis. The police. I rush to my bedroom and hide under the blankets. I imagine my trial and my prison cell. The fear is terrifying. All of a sudden, you're nothing anymore. I curse myself. But I can hear laughter. The policemen are just colleagues of my father calling to say hello: little Burtin, who would one day place a ticket on his own car after having had one aperitif too many, and tall Tousseau, with his nose that looks like de Gaulle's. I creep downstairs. I'm still a bit frightened. You never know. It may be a cunning trick designed to arrest whoever vandalised the barrel of tar. But no, the police van is driving away. It's time to eat. My mother has laid the table. I wash my hands with soap and discover a black smear on my left forearm. Greasy and sticky, it refuses to budge, and it even spreads further as if to proclaim that I am guilty. Guilty.

Pink sandstone

THE LOW HOUSES OF THE VOSGES, AT THE END OF the long autumn afternoons, in the sparse light and the rain-washed cold. A foolish wind. Stubborn. That nothing can halt, neither the overhanging roofs, nor the umbrellas that get soaked when we lay flowers in the cemeteries on All Saints Day. Celles-sur-Plaine. Saint-Blaise. Châtas. The course of our dead ones. The trail of chrysanthemums. We drive through deserted valleys in which silent villages slumber beneath thick forests of dark fir trees. The fountains spout murky water. Reddish. The cafés are at half mast. Nothing stirs. I don't dare move either in the house where my grandmother, my father's mother, Clémentine lives; a pretty name for a woman who never smiles and shows no affection. We stay in her kitchen, which is the place where she receives, eats, dozes, keeps time at bay, and sees out her days and her life. I've never been into her bedroom and shall never see it. Her deathbed, where I shall give her a final kiss, will be upstairs in the house of her daughter, Aunt Nénette, my father's twin sister. I'm bored. It's so cold. There's no heating. It's too early. November has barely begun. The dead leaves beneath the trees are gathering like penitents. My mother is bored too, she says very little, and my father and his mother, unconcerned about us, reel off the litany of legacies, of old resentments, the possessions sold by others, the gossip and the family affairs that are more usually tinged with hatred than love. I close my eyes. I try to understand the smell of the house, as though I might like it better if I did. Dampness, saltpetre, mildew, well-inked newspaper that is not thrown away because it will be used to wipe arses, a stench of straw, of clothes that never properly dry. Old smoke. Stale tart that is beginning to decay in its black tin. It's a lair, a cavern. All that is lacking is the moss, the stalactites, the concretions, the bats. My speleology leads me only to terror, that of being condemned to live there and yet, and yet, I'm curiously drawn to the water stone, carved from a single block of pink sandstone, that flesh of the Vosges that is constantly drenched since cheerful water dribbles from the tap. It's rather like having a spring in one's house where the water oozes from a cut in the earth. And this sandstone, which is the colour of girls' lips, when it drips perpetually in this way, offers whoever touches it, strokes it and drinks from it, an almost floral scent – sweet, forest-like and delicate – and possessing a lightness that in spite of the compact, heavy mass of the barely eroded stone is as old as the world itself.

Gym

GYMS POSSESS AN UNRECOGNISED EROTIC POWER.
Especially those old-fashioned ones in which dust, lack of ventilation, shabby walls, chlorotic light and decrepit changing-rooms have combined to produce, paradoxically, a suitable setting for the kindling of amorous desire. Père Georges is our sports teacher. We are in our fifth year at the Lycée Bichat in Lunéville. He smokes a great deal, hasn't run for a long time, and the premises that he shares with his colleagues resemble the annexe of a brewery. I think he has considered the problem from all angles and his couldn't-care-less attitude is not the least of the lessons he has taught us. There are quite a few of us, in any case, who happen to be slow movers, who have certainly not forgotten this. The class at the lycée is a mixed one, but for physical education and sports, the girls go their way and we go ours. Lacework doesn't mix with coarse woollen cloth. We happen, however, to share the same gym. They in one corner, we in another, we take turns leaping over the

same vaulting-horses, we grasp the same parallel bars, rings, knotted ropes and horizontal bars, we tumble onto the same mattresses, we roll on the same floor-mats. Our taut young bodies keep brushing up against one another. We look at these girls, whom we know so well, in a new light. We breathe in the strain that moistens their foreheads and their armpits, that lends a vague and languorous weariness to their expressions, a sensual sluggishness to their movements, a warmth to their breath that seems intended to arouse us whenever we catch it. Their cheeks flush. In a flash they are not girls in a budding grove, but are instead ablaze, and this fire is making us glow. Père Georges may stink of beer, Pernod and tobacco, the gym may reek of sweat, feet and unwashed bodies, the dilapidated condition of the actual ropes and the mats – whose crumbling rubber foam curiously emits a scented hint of gum arabic – may give the place a Soviet atmosphere, but in no way does any of it prevent me from being excited by Corinne Remoux's thighs, flecked on their insides with a downy *sfumato*, by the auburn charms of Carole Ravaillé, by the unforgettable breasts – well-developed for her age – of Marie Marin, by the pubis, lithe as an otter's belly, of blonde Isabelle Leclerc, whose tiny, navy-blue, padded shorts reveal as much as they conceal. I am intoxicated by everything. I revel in the chuckling, the jostling, the low necklines, the pink or white gleam of knickers that can occasionally be glimpsed in the scissor movement of thighs when a girl does the high jump, the quivering of two breasts during a run-up, the brief sight of a backside when she does the splits, the flexing of knees when a girl is coiled on the rope, as she slithers elegantly upwards, her back bent, panting gently, towards the roof of the gym, while I stand open-mouthed, my eyes transported, my brain clouded by the surge of hormones, my prick as hard as a piece of Roman marble. Gyms have remained old friends of mine. They understand. Some people still hold their noses as they enter and make a face. In my case, I close my eyes. I'm looking for the girls. My girls. I can actually hear them, laughing and teasing one another, running around and spurring each other on, but I no longer see them. They are locked away in a time warp, and I am moving on.

Fried bacon

AT THE END OF OUR GARDEN, NEAR THE CHICKEN run, my father occasionally erects a smokehouse, consisting of a sheet of zinc rolled in on itself and surmounted with a tube-shaped chimney. He hangs long strips of raw bacon inside it and beneath them he places spadefuls of ground spruce that burns slowly, without flames, producing a bluish smoke similar to the clouds that rise up when the woodcutters are at work in the fir plantations during the autumn, hovering on the crests of the tall trees as though to crown them. From the forests of the Vosges comes a typical Vosgian joke: "Do you like your father or your mother best? – I like bacon best!" It takes many days for the smoking to take effect. When my father removes the strips, they have become shrivelled and hardened, and they have exchanged their fresh pink-and-white colour for others that are more muted, the rind has turned to leather, and if you put your nose near it, the smell of the meat has now blended with the wild scent of the conifer and the fumigation. Take a well-sharpened knife, a chopping board, cut off two slices half a centimetre thick from the strip of bacon, heat a pan, place a small knob of butter in it, wait for it to melt and then lay the two slices flat. Music and pleasure. The kitchen starts to buzz with the crackling of the flesh while at the same time, from the pan, a thick plume of smoke is released that smells of warm fat, grilled meat, pine cones and singed hair. We gaze at the rapid mutations of the bacon with the fatty parts becoming translucent and moist from the heat, whereas the streaks of lean meat turn Tyrian pink, mauve, ruby-red, even a sienna if the cooking continues. Withdraw the pan. Lay the two rashers on some farmhouse bread. Dribble some burning oil over them. Eat while hot. My father is preparing this for me. No diet recommends this recipe and more is the pity. It is, however, one of the paths that leads to perfect happiness. The smell of bacon frying, along with that of fried onions, or the two combined, induces instant salivation in me and a sense of bliss that endures long after the meal. It would be more suitable as a snack. Something improvised, simply, without fuss, at about ten o'clock in the morning, as though to poke fun at normal accepted behaviour. On returning from the market, for example, on Thursdays – having walked past Père Haffner, the pork butcher and pig breeder from Montigny, not far from the Donon region, as he lays out his stall (it's rather like gazing into a toyshop window before Christmas) – I set down my treasures on the kitchen table. I have brawn, black pudding, white pudding with *trompettes-de-la-mort* mushrooms, smoked bacon, snout, saveloys, chipolatas, crumbed trotters, ham on the bone, filet mignon – and, in order to pay homage to the sacrificial beast and to whoever sacrificed it, I grab the bacon, sniff it, cut off two thin slices, prepare the bread and the pan, as my father used to do for me and, after pouring myself a glass of Santenay from Borgeot's shop, I get ready to celebrate the Mass that I am not prepared to forego.

Vegetables

YOU ONLY HAVE TO PUSH OPEN THE DOOR WITH the shop bell at the bottom of rue Jeanne d'Arc, not far from where it crosses rue Mathieu. And you walk into a vegetable garden assembled in a space the size of a handkerchief. It doesn't hold many people. What's more, few are hurrying to get in. They send me there in the spring for a packet of seeds, or a large slice of pumpkin in late September, for a bundle of leeks when we need some, for three warty colcynths to look pretty on the sideboard, for new carrots tied in a bunch with raffia when our own are late, for a lettuce still moist with dew. The place smells of soup, but before any cooking has begun, when the housewife's hands have gathered together all the vegetables, rid them of their muddy skins and chopped them up, releasing their aromas, their saps, their essence of turnip or leek. A stupendous *pot-au-feu*, raw and with no meat. The Vincents' shop is a large cauldron beneath which the flame has not yet been lit. The mother is bent over, a tiny, inoffensive witch, a grey shrew, alarmingly thin and as wrinkled as an elephant's hide. The son is enormous and so ruddy he looks fit to explode. And he will explode one day. He has the face of a Minotaur. I think he's splendid and mythological. Pity he has two eyes, or he would be Polyphemus. I recognise him in certain simple and basic Picasso drawings, sketched at a single stroke. They say he drinks. That he's often at the Deux Roues and at other bars. That he ends up lying on the floor, asleep. So what? What is sold there comes from the soil and from their four industrious, cracked hands, from their courage and their patience. Their gardens are long, dark strips behind the cemetery. All the vegetables grow next to the dead, who pass on some of their memory to them: potatoes, cabbages – red, white, curly, plain, Brussels sprouts – chard, cardoons, beetroot, onions, asparagus, tomatoes, turnips, salsify, shallots, garlic, sorrel, white and black radishes, batavias and other lettuces, oak leaves, endives, chicory, lamb's lettuce, *pouyottes*, herbs displayed in a blue amethyst vase, in little bunches, chervil, flat-leaved and curly-leaved parsley, tarragon, thyme, rosemary, spring onions, sage, savory. A still-life that is more Flemish, generous and fragrant, a huge basket of living and fabulous smells which, depending on the season, varies its flavours so as to prepare for the sweet, autumnal splendours when fruit and vegetables gradually make way for each other. When old mother Vincent dies, her son barely survives her. He succumbs all of a sudden, like a large stricken oak tree. For a few months after their deaths, the little shop keeps its window filled with pot plants that eventually dry up and die because there is no-one left to water them. Sale. Purchase. The new owners fill the entrance in and rebuild it. Nothing remains of the original shop. Opposite it, the big Boussac workshop, which used to employ over a thousand seamstresses, has been transformed into curious apartments separated by fences, in front of which are small gardens, each of them boasting a table, four plastic chairs and a barbecue. A little further away, the concert hall and the Jeanne d'Arc cinema have closed down for good. "The shape of a town changes more quickly, alas, than the heart of a human being." Baudelaire yet again. Who had clearly understood everything there is to understand about objects and humankind.

Childhood home

IT'S THE 17TH OF NOVEMBER 2011 AND I'M SITTING
at the kitchen table. Outside, it is several degrees below zero.
It's drizzling. It's the kind of grey day I like. In two hours' time,
dusk will have fallen. The house has been unoccupied for over
two years. Ever since my father's death. It has been partially
cleared of furniture and cleaned. Many things still lie scattered
around: pieces of furniture, open cardboard boxes, piles of
plates, plastic bags that have begun to be filled with medicines,
paperwork and various objects. My father's bed has been taken
away. He broke it stumbling backwards onto it one morning
on his way back from getting his coffee. There are brooms left
lying untouched. A rather bored-looking vacuum cleaner has
the whole of the sitting room to itself. The house resembles a
dead person who has been half-washed and then left in that
condition, not for any particular reason, not out of weariness
or neglect, but simply because there were other things to do.
I hesitated a long time before coming to write this chapter

here, at this very table where, as a child, I did my homework; in this kitchen that hasn't changed much and where we used to eat our meals and play Monopoly and other board games with my sisters Brigitte and Nathalie and my parents. It's very cold in this house today. It's not heated. Nobody lives here anymore. It's the house of a dead man, and my father in his grave, on the far side of the road, less than two hundred metres away, can scarcely be any colder than I am. If I look up, I can see the landscape of my childhood once more through the windows. The gardens are still there, but they have been left untended. The men and women who stubbornly cultivated them died a long time ago. I mention their names so that they should not be entirely forgotten: le grand Hoquart, Madame Cahour, Madame and Monsieur Herbeth, Monsieur Méline, Monsieur Lebon. Our neighbours, the Morettis, the Claudes, the Ripplings, the Finots. That's about it. The pond is still there, the fields, the Sânon river, the Grand Canal and, beyond, the Rambêtant river, which vanishes into the mist and the sky. Someone has parked a caravan behind the lane. An incongruous splash of white and yellow. I wonder what sort of traveller it can be waiting for. But perhaps they have decided to leave it there, just as some people attempt to lose their dog when they grow tired of it. I visit the rooms. I go in through the garage, after having removed the three screws that my father, in his troubled final days, attached to the door. I rediscover the smell of petrol, drains, workshop, oil-can, leather straps, saddlery. On the workbench, written on a slat of wood, is Einstein's saying: "Order is the virtue of the mediocre", which had become a convenient motto of his. I'm coming back home, to familiar territory. But after that, nothing more. I go upstairs, to the kitchen, bedroom, sitting room. I open the shutters. I go to the attic, walk through my elder sister's bedroom, and I come to the loft that my father converted when I was thirteen. My bedroom. My domain, which, once I had left home, became my little sister's. Pine panels on the walls and the ceiling, a desk made of the same wood, green carpet on the floor. I like this place. It reminds me of the mountain refuges that fire my imagination and that I would visit frequently later on. It's here that I have my first erection. It's here that I masturbate for the first time, dreaming of my German teacher's breasts in year three. Here that I smoke my first cigarette. Here that I watch Claude-Jean Philippe's Ciné-club over the years on an old black-and-white television set, and thus it is here, beneath these rafters, that I encounter Jean Grémillon, Julien Duvivier, Ernst Lubitsch, Frank Capra, Federico Fellini and a few others. The same apologetic cold dampens all the rooms and even though I sniff the air for a long time, blow my nose frequently to unblock my nostrils, and close my eyes, I can't smell a thing. Nothing. The house no longer smells of anything. My father has departed taking with him the distinctive flavour of this building. He is dead, and the smell of the house has died too. I feel cold. It's the first time I have written here for many years. For over thirty years, I think. It's also the last time. Soon, the house will be sold, repainted, altered. Human beings will live in it, they will bring their own lives, their dreams, their sadnesses, their anxieties and their tranquillity. They will sleep here, make love here, wash, go to the bathrooms, mend things, they will cry, laugh, bring up their children. Gradually, like soft wax, the house will mould itself to them, and retain their smells. I know that when I go past it, on my bicycle or in a car, I won't look at it. I won't be able to. On my way to Sommerviller, I shall prefer to turn my head to the right, towards the cemetery, towards the dead, towards my father. It's sad not to smell anything anymore. It's sad being there, in the cold house that has lost its fragrance rather as Peter Schlemihl lost his shadow in the children's tale. I thought I would feel moved. I even thought I might cry, crying easily as I do. But no. I am merely surprised. Astonished. I don't know whether it is I who have changed course or whether it's the house. But we are now like two strangers to one another. It's my fault, after all. No-one forced me to go back there. I shall leave. I shall close the shutters, turn off the lights, shut the doors, replace the three screws. I shall return to the world of the living again. I no longer have my place here. I've just understood this. I've also just sneezed. If I stay any longer, I feel I'll catch a cold. Where I come from, they say "catch a death".

Death

FOR A LONG TIME DEATH WAS A HOME-LOVER. YOU died in your own home, you lay there on display for a few days, and then you crossed the threshold for the last time. The dead person's bed was often the one in which he was born, had dreams, made love, and spent all his sleepless or peaceful nights. I saw my first dead person when I was fourteen. It was a dead woman, in actual fact: my paternal grandmother, whom I did not much care for. That's probably the reason why the sight of the shrivelled, laid-out body with its pinched lips barely moved me. The main thing I remember is having been interested. It was a lesson in life. An initiation. I lean forwards briefly, scanning her waxy parchment skin as though with a magnifying glass or the lens of a microscope. Only when my lips touch her cheeks do I shudder. Death has caught up with me. The face is hard and cold. It has the appearance of a human, but the indifference and hardness of a mineral substance. Fear causes me to shed a few tears, which are probably misinterpreted. Not long ago, it was my father's cheeks that I kissed. My fourteen years are long gone now and I have stopped counting the dead. Stopped being afraid, too. My father is in the morgue, which is no longer called a morgue by the way, but a "funeral parlour", in keeping with the mendacity of our age. Velvet curtains, dimmed lights, soft music, sprays of flowers. The odour of death is no longer that of the dead man's bedroom, where you can still recognise him, smell him. At the morgue, all the dead are mingled together. They all have a scent of exuberant tuberose, air-conditioning, cosmetics. My father, like all the others before him, like my Uncle Dédé, has become sovietised. Brezhnev-like. I scarcely recognise him. A creature touched up for the official portrait and the mausoleum. Yellow. Powdered. Smoothed over. Eyebrows combed. Kremlin and Red Square. In short, one great lie. When I kiss him, I can't recognise his smell at all. He reeks of woman and of medicine. An odd mixture of formalin and powdered rice, of make-up and camphorated lotion. Death shuffles the cards. She even deals first. She anticipates. My mother has prepared for her death. She has paid in instalments at no extra charge. All the details are finalised. The clerk went through them with me on the phone not long ago. He spoke to me about the flowers, the music, the coffin, about embalming the body, since one didn't know what condition my mother would be in. My mother was sitting beside him, still very much alive, and was listening to him describing her future corpse. I felt trapped. Gridlocked. They were both drinking champagne. He had brought a bottle to celebrate the contract.

Death clearly thinks of everything, adapts to the times, changes attire. It innovates. One can understand. It, too, must get bored. Winning every time isn't much of a contest.

Munster

BANISHED. EXPELLED. DOOMED TO BE KEPT ON the window sill in summer or winter, come rain or snow. Yet it's insignificant in appearance, small, round, not very thick, hovering between yellow and orange, and bearing scabs of white or grey mould in places. Once opened, and if still young, it reveals a chalky-white texture that has the pallor of a Norman cliff and crumbles easily at the touch of a knife. Over time, it acquires a softness and can even start to ooze, becoming ochre-coloured and shiny while its crust creases like the over-powdered cheeks of a lady of private means. My mother won't tolerate its presence in the fridge and is appalled whenever my father, for whom it is both a delicacy and Proust's *petite madeleine*, secretly brings one into the house. "You don't know what's good," he tells her. To which she replies: "You're quite right, otherwise I wouldn't have married you!" My mother doesn't like it, and therefore neither do I or my sisters. That's why it has taken me so long to try not only this cheese, but goats' cheeses, brains and leg of lamb, all of which I now enjoy greatly. I follow my mother's tastes blindly, and like her I disapprove of my father's degenerate taste for foul-smelling foods. I pretend to look horrified. I hold my nose, make faces and look as though I want to throw up. The Munster ages outside, homeless, a milky-white tramp sheltering wretchedly against a folded shutter, beneath the haughty gaze of the thermometer. When, at the end of the meal, my father gets up to invite it to the table, we leave the kitchen, yelling loudly like those idiotic and unruly members of parliament who storm out of the Assemblée Nationale. So it is on his own that my father envelops himself in the fumes of the unspeakable, unmentionable thing, the thing that has no place in our house or in our language, and which bears a legend, put about by its enemies, stating that in order to mature it must be urinated upon, which is untrue because the poor cheese-maker would have to pee far too much. Liquefied manure, slurry, fluid shit, silent fart, sour cream, decayed tooth, if smelling it is difficult, it's in the mouth that it comes into its own. To smell it is to condemn it, to taste it is to pardon it. Behind its Quasimodo, ugly-duckling, scabrous appearance, it is like a prince waiting for the right person to appreciate him before he can reveal himself. We are so often mistaken, about cheeses and human beings.

Umbellifers

YOU ARE ABOUT TO ENTER INTO A SANCTUARY. SO it is advisable to bow your head. As though to a queen. A queen of the fields and the meadows, of those fantastical, grassy June expanses. What fragrance would you take to a desert island that had none of its own? All those I mention, certainly, but this one, which connects me through mysterious ties to my earliest experience of the world, more than any other. I spent my childhood in a state of constant bedazzlement, nature accompanying each of my transformations by revealing a new secret to me. The secret of birds, fishes, rodents, flowers, trees, rocks, waters. The secret of the days and the seasons, the clouds, the meteors, the mists and the constellations. There is so much to learn and to take in. I absorb. With my eyes closed, I walk through the fallow field. It's late June and the weather is rainy and gentle, almost hot. School is over. A large greenhouse has settled over the countryside, its nutritive condensation protecting the banks of the Sânon, the Rambêtant, and the closest of the Sommerviller farms whose roofs I can see in the distance. A steam bath. Behind the wispy clouds, the sun refuses to set. The grass, already tall, is soaked. With each step I make, it dries itself against my thighs, leaving warm drops that drip down inside my boots. I stroke it with my hands. I close my eyes. I don't want to see, just to smell. The water. The springtime. The scent of moist earth, impatiently waiting to welcome new shoots. I search. I know they're very near. I want to be the victim of their spell once more. They are the sirens of the meadows. They seduce the walker with their green exhalations of dill, and afterwards the poor fellow can't enjoy other herbs, haunted as he is forever more by their cumin-like fragrance in which, faintly, sporadic hints of aniseed and clove can be detected. Umbellifers. And the utterly feminine name in French – *ombellifères* – with its male syllable ending is like a fairy-tale open sesame. I mumble it as I walk. I say it over again. *Ombellifères. Ombellifères.* A large head crowned with small flowers already arranged like a bouquet, a graceful plume of the kind I shall discover later on in the opalescent glassworks and the russet marquetry of Emile Gallé, and whose scents unravel in the air, rather like those complicated corsets that once imprisoned girls' impatient bodies and the heavier, languid and more sensual ones belonging to their mothers.

Fishing trousers

A CRUST OF BREAD AS HARD AS AGATE IN THE MIDDLE, but crumbling at the edges, a shortened bit of shoelace, shrivelled, brittle and black, which, after more careful examination, proves to be the dried body of a worm, a small fistful of clay soil reduced to dust, a melted and now hardened La Pie qui chante sweet, the chocolate coating of which varies from grey to brown, a cap from a beer bottle, a paper handkerchief, rolled in a ball, covered with dozens of fish scales that have lost their lustre and shine, a reel of line, breaking strain of 800 grams, about ten small lead sinkers, a broken red and yellow balsa-wood float used for small fish, the remains of a ham sandwich, in aluminium foil, that's curiously intact, though inedible, an envelope containing an electricity bill and its payment, which has never been posted, a few dead maggots, oblong, solid and dark, and which look like mice droppings, three strips of chlorophyll chewing-gum, a burst tube of Rubifix, a thin roll of pink toilet paper, Machiavelli's *The Prince* in an old schoolbook edition, a completely chewed pencil three centimetres long, a pebble the size of a duck's egg, perfectly flat and ideal for skimming, a shopping list – "pasta, butter, curly lettuce, matches, cordial, three pork loin chops, 60-watt bulbs, road salt, don't forget the eggs!" – for goods that I'm not sure were ever purchased, an elastic band, the paper that some Charlot bait was wrapped in and which has retained its smell of aniseed. End of the inventory. The trousers have four deep, baggy pockets at the front. They have lost their colour. One day, long ago, when they were new and recently designed, they were probably khaki or celadon, although celadon strikes me as an inappropriate colour for a pair of fishing trousers, but I remind myself they weren't always used for fishing and that by using them in this way I am actually giving them a second life, a sort of active retirement, a belated professional career change. They are appallingly stained, in an inexplicable way, and dirty. They can only ever be dirty in any case, and chilly, too, for I refuse to have them washed and I leave them lying around in an unheated hut at the end of our garden. When I put them on after a few months, they're as stiff as a Breton fisherman's sou'wester, and I sometimes construe this reluctant rigidity as a reproach. But I like them like this, rugged, filthy, stuffed with masses of objects that are both evidence of their being used and of their owner's absent-mindedness. Some would imagine they stink. In fact they don't smell at all, and this is very strange given all I put them through, and considering all the things they accommodate. I'd even forgotten that I left a dead fish inside them. I found it again, weeks later, dehydrated and virtually odourless, curiously like a dagger with lacklustre eyes. What these torn, patched-up, worn-out trousers, stuffed with an assortment of strange oddities, smell of is the astonishing odour of a flour-mill, of the back-room of a windmill, of ground grain and bran. But their true smell is that of a bounding and joyful heart. A smell of the great outdoors, of life without constrictions, of free time, far from everything, far from everyone, beside rivers, in puzzling dialogue with the water and its reflections, with its depths that are an echo of my own depths. Murky or clear, by turns.

Swimming pool

ON A COLD WINTER AFTERNOON, AT ABOUT FIVE o'clock, when the daylight is already fading and dissolving into a wash of metal filings and ashes, we decide to go to the circular swimming pool at Nancy-thermal. We walk through the glass doors and the sulphur mugginess hits us, like a sickly, all-enveloping, full-blown embrace. We buy our tickets from the lady at the counter who, enclosed in her glass box, and unaware of the fact, makes us reflect on the cruelty of fate, in a way we would normally think of goldfish. We make our way along the narrow corridor and in the distance we can hear the echo of voices beneath the dome, sounding further away, but also fainter than in real life, as well as the splash of water thrown up by the swimmers and the sound of children playing. We go into a cabin. We undress, as though we were removing a succession of skins, layers of clothing that we hang on the hook. It's freezing or snowing outside, and in a matter of moments we're naked. There's a mischievousness about the procedure, an agreeable counter-flow that encourages a slight sense of freedom and rebellion. We have put on our swimming costumes and we go out through another door, for here the cabins are the unmanned frontier posts between two opposing countries, the one tiled, windowless and dry, the other liquid and filled with a light that descends from a glass roof in the sky onto blue water that, at the edges of the pool, is iridescent with green, beige and grey, and is overlooked by a balustrade built of *flambé* sandstone from Rambervillers. Curvaceous and healing. For the swimming pool is circular and its water is thermal. People splash around there rather than swim. They laugh, they chat, they prattle away. Life there is conjoined at either end: you come across old people and babies who, in their mothers' arms, are discovering liquid warmth and its caress. In this nave without an altar, the air seems to murmur, and the words, the babbling, slip out of the immense round belly in which one floats, reflecting on the invisible source that, from beneath the crust of the earth supplies this beneficent water with its medicinal, stagnant stench, and to which a drop of chlorine lends a slightly irritating sensation that both arouses and exhilarates. It's always warmer here than in other pools elsewhere, so much so that I can spend a long time in the water without fear of getting cold, in a relative weightless state that suits the fluctuations of the spirit, the detachment, the reverie and the confusing manifestations of writing. You can forget Nancy. You're in Budapest, or in Prague, somewhere far away in the heart of Europe and part of history. You delve back to moments that preceded the great slaughters, to the time of royal families and horse-drawn carriages, and the bracing steam of the water allows the ghosts of Toscani-smoking chess-players and pot-bellied men, taking the waters and discussing the Triple Alliance, to hover there within easy reach.

Pissotières

I HAVE TO TRAVEL A VERY LONG WAY TO FIND ANY *pissotières*. French cities abolished the right to urinate free of charge long ago. An urban property developer had evidently remembered the Emperor Vespasian's method. Once again, they taxed micturition, and people had to give a coin instead of paying in liquid cash. What's more, these ugly automatic cabins whose doors close with the hiss of a guillotine have nothing in common with the public conveniences that once adorned parks, public gardens and pavements. You are appallingly alone inside them. Solitary, unable to see the light of day or hear the swishing of your neighbour busy doing the same thing as you. I like the old-fashioned architecture of *pissotières*, the slender, almost modish, ornate ironwork, with its supple curves, or else the solid stone structures, sometimes made of bare concrete, but indestructible and comforting. You're not far from passers-by when you urinate there. You can hear the noises of the town that you have momentarily left behind. You can exchange

unimportant remarks. Some people give vent to explicit or
abstruse graffiti – I remember, in particular a mysterious
"Grelot, I'll have your shit" – others arrange meetings there,
chat people up, and sometimes make love there in a rough and
hurried manner. It's one of the arguments the great minds put
forward for closing many of them. The powerful stenches that
emanate from them don't bother me, nor do the stains they
are sometimes smeared with. You know you're not entering a
flower shop when you walk in. Rancid urine, excrement, Cresyl
and Javel disinfectants create miasmas that could feature in
the litany of our wretchedness. It's a way of understanding
ethics at no cost. Breathing in such smells teaches us humility
and contrition. Our world longs to be odourless, that is to say
inhuman. In the centuries that preceded our own, everything
smelled, both the good and the bad. We drive away smells, those
from our bodies and those from our cities, like base delinquents
who might overly remind us that we produce humours and that
they stink. As a boy, I would walk into a *pissotière* and it reeked. I
wasn't surprised or embarrassed. I would come across a certain
kind of mirror that didn't distort much. I would learn who I
was. Sometimes, there was a tramp snoring there, gracing the
restricted space with his effluvia of cheap wine, filth and shag
tobacco. I would imagine him to be a god fallen among men,
masking his true nature beneath his tattered rags. For Zeus,
after all, occasionally changes himself into a swan or a cow. So
why might I not come across him disguised as a vagrant, sitting
on his arse in a *pissotière*, snoring happily to the buzz of the
flies? But nowadays we have also done away with the gods.

Rainstorm

YOU COULD BANG YOUR FIST ON THE EARTH AS you might bang it on the table. We've been waiting so long for the fight to begin. For days and days the sky had been filled with a heavy lead and a heat that stunted the horizon, shackled the wind, and made people and animals feel restless. There had been no coolness even at night, which was just like daytime, affected by the obscene palpation of a mugginess that seemed to believe it belonged everywhere and at all times. Windows are left open to no avail. And then, in the early afternoon, the sky to the north over the Seille country seems to grow taut and start to rustle. Subdued glimmers can be seen, as in a sort of stuttering apocalypse. Everything grows dark. I'm reminded of those Good Fridays when we wait to see how the storm clouds will commemorate the Crucified Man of Golgotha. A crash of light and fury. The thunderbolt's axe strikes a willow tree by the pond. We hadn't seen it coming. A tree split in two, twitching, revealing its white flesh from top to bottom, like a pale thigh emerging from a torn stocking. Thunder strikes again, three hundred metres further to the left, on an electric pylon. Hysterical streaks of lightning. The passing signature of a megalomaniac artist. The heifers in Poulet's field hurtle off and charge towards the river, only to pause again, foolishly, at the top of the embankment, where they come to a halt. A murmur. That grows louder. It's the rain which, having caused the banks of the Rambêtant to vanish under a streaked screen, rushes through the air like a tide, engulfs the coppices beside the Grand Canal, soaks up the fields, slips away towards our house and is already streaming over the back gardens. The cat glides under the flat stone propped awkwardly against the rabbit hutches. Isolated drops provide the first dull notes, just by the chicken-run, and then the bulk of it arrives, a slanting and weighty ill-disciplined army that slashes shamelessly at the last of the tulip petals, shreds the still delicate leaves of the cherry trees, humiliates the peonies by forcing them to bow their creamy heads before crushing them to the ground, while the hailstones create millions of craters the size of a thumbnail in the ground. An elemental massacre. A bombardment. A cataract. The water refreshes the air and slices through it. It's the snout of a monster blowing its hot tropical breath straight in our faces. Muddy waters stream in miniature rivers along the footpaths, and shimmering pools form at the foot of the raspberry canes. Sheltered from the storm, people shiver slightly, and they smile as they sniff the wafts the destruction has brought, humus from the marshlands, peat, sap, seeds from the corollas of lilies with weeping petals like rags, hairs from the agitated cattle mooing in chorus in the distance, bubbles of silt blown up by the ripple of new lavender whose growth has been stimulated by the storm, resin come from nobody knows where, and once the wind has arisen at last, it takes its revenge and fans all this with the last drops of rain as it drives the jumble of exhausted clouds and the thunderclaps towards the east, where for the time being it is still peaceful.

Fish

MINNOW. GUDGEON. TENCH. CHUB. BLEAK. NOSE-carp. Barbel. Trout. Carp. Bream. Perch. Sander. Pike. Dace. Rudd. Fishes' bodies are supple and smooth, teeming with electric energy. They glide through the water, gently driven by the mucus that infuses the fisherman's hand with a scent of fountains and watercress, freshness and sweet-smelling shells, kelp and the open sea – and this is true even for those who swim in rivers. In order to try to understand the mystery of fishing you have to have inhaled it. You need to be there, on the river bank, at the moment that the wriggling body of the fish caught on a hook springs from the surface of the stream. To soothe it. Not squeeze it too tightly in your fingers, to lay it on the grass if necessary, to remove as carefully as possible the thin bit of metal from its open mouth. A round eye, encircled with gold, is watching you. And is considering you reproachfully. It glistens, like the rest of the creature's body, a pure gem, delicate and refined in its tear-shaped bronze markings and its shades of green, blue and grey. For years, I would dream of this event and of this smell. It never happened. I would spend hours without managing to catch a single fish on the banks of the Meurthe, the Petit Canal, the Poncé pond, or else at the Goulotte du Sânon: out of its large drainpipe came all the blood from the abattoirs a little higher upstream, nowadays the premises of the fire station. The thick blood of the cattle, the horses and the pigs, bright red or brown, and sometimes clotted, flowed down the stream where it stained the water over several metres. Large crimson clouds could be seen rolling along in the murky currents before they dissolved. Fish revel in the blood of the dead. On the days when great slaughters were planned, room was scarce and you had to get up early in order to mark out your territory and unpack your rods. It was there that I eventually caught my first roach, my first *rousse*, as we say here. Vermilion fins. Smooth scales. A smell of algae and deepness. A first miracle. A poem of moist scales. A fish of silvery rhymes, that I sniffed at for a long time, my heart thumping, just as an animal smells another animal, without modesty or shame.

Ointment

MY CHILDHOOD WAS THAT OF AN INVALID'S. IN the past, I would no doubt have made a very pretty little dead child, no sooner baptised than immediately buried in the small patch of white graves dotted with plaster cherubs in our cemetery. I survived thanks to advances in medicine. I chose the right century. I often used to see Doctor Joachim Meyer-Bisch, who has the fine face of a philosopher, solemn spectacles and incisors that push back his upper lip, rather like the marvellous actor Jean Bouise whom I regret to this day never having met. The waiting room at his surgery is comfortable. I feel at ease there. The imitation leather chairs stick to my bottom. The shelves of his bookcase only contain incomprehensible works. Discreet loudspeakers broadcast symphonies and sonatas. His hands touch my forehead, my stomach, my chest. He listens to my heart and looks at my throat, but he never strokes my balls unlike that doctor from my father's health insurance company who wanted to check whether I was able to go away to holiday camp. At that time, it was very important that one's balls should have dropped to where they were meant to have dropped in order to be allowed to go away to holiday camp. Our parents could see no reason to object. Doctor Joachim Meyer-Bisch has a German name, but he's inoffensive. He has nothing in common with those who killed my great-uncles and cousins in 1915, or set fire to our farms, and, in 1942, deported, gassed and then burned my mother's little friends, the Lazarovitch sisters, as well as their entire family, with the exception of one of their brothers. He wears a white coat, which he buttons to the very top, but when he calls at our house because my temperature is too high for me to be moved, he wears a suit, tie and a V-necked pullover. I can still see his pen with its gold nib, his leather bag from which he takes out his stethoscope and his prescription pad. He is neither nice nor unpleasant. He is the Doctor. He has a large family whom he drives around in a large Mercedes. Monsieur Gorius, the chemist, also has a Mercedes, but his family can't be very big because his car only has two seats. One day, Monsieur Gorius asks me to choose between a cough syrup or an ointment for haemorrhoids, since I don't have enough money to pay for both of them. A dilemma which Corneille never used as an excuse for one of his plays, and he ought to have done: should one give preference to making the throat feel better or to the serenity of the anus? The ointment must be for my father. I leave without anything. My mother is furious. We change chemists. Ointment. The very word makes me feel virtually cured. I like all ointments. The tube or the small brown glass pots in which they are held captive, their creamy, sometimes sticky, smoothness, their colours of pale make-up, and most of all their fragrances of eucalyptus, camphor and mustard. My mother comes to see me, she sits on the edge of my bed, unbuttons my pyjama top. She puts a little ointment on her fingertips and warms it before applying it gently, by means of a delicate massage, to my torso, which is nothing but skin and bone. I can immediately feel the beneficial burning sensation as, simultaneously, the intense smell of a forest brimming with the scents of resin and menthol invades my bedroom. Thanks to this aroma, thanks to the warm sting of the ointment penetrating my congested lungs, and to my mother's affectionate presence on this day off, once again, I shan't be going to school, but can instead read to my heart's content and doze, and dream, and see my mother at those times of day when she is normally alone. I feel better already.

Prison

PRISON IS AN ENCLOSED CAULDRON IN WHICH
bodies, souls, dreams, remorse and anger all stew. Weeks,
months and years of detention. People eat there. They sleep
there. They learn there. They forget there. They brood there.
They do away with themselves there. They come to grief
there. They recover there. They defecate there. They masturbate
there. Sometimes they sodomise each other there. They try
to kill time there. But, for all that, prison is not a vile place.
We have created it. It is built in our image. It is to mankind,
in short, what quintessence is to fragrance: a concentrated
absolute. For almost twelve years, I used to visit a prison several
times a week to give lessons. Up until 2000. Ever since, it has
dwelled within the depths of my being, my awareness, and my
judgement as well, and it won't leave them. I don't have any
intention of trying to get rid of it either. Prison is one of those
places that possesses its own odour: the hospital – something
slightly refrigerated; the old people's home – clear soup and

inert bodies; the gym – perspiring feet, sweat, the rubbery foam of floor mats. Prison is just such a place. To be witty, an idiot might say that it smells of mould. He would not be entirely wrong. Let us say, instead, it smells of confinement, of being shut away. That state that is totally inimical with the human species, which by definition is nomadic, explorative, itinerant and free. Prison life – and the very principle of imprisonment – produces behaviour that is specific to it, pathologies that you encounter nowhere else, and distinct odours. Everything there is lacklustre, subdued, paralysed and things which, in the outside world, can be indulged in freely stagnate within the thick walls, beneath the high glass roofs, and in the wretched exercise area behind bars. Restrained, reduced, diluted, the fragrances of life are an octave lower in prison. They fade away and are unable to resonate as they should. Scarcely have they come in, than they decompose and dissolve. They take on the patina of old walls, the grime of floors that are nevertheless constantly washed, the weary sadness of paint that is reapplied in vain every spring. Like the people who live alongside them, the smells no longer make any effort to show off or dress themselves. They surrender their distinctive features, resign themselves and become uniform. And that is probably what most characterises the stench of this place, which is at once a part of our world while at the same time not part of it: the smells refuse to be what they are and to stand out from one another. They let themselves slip into a state of neglect. They give up. The smell of prison is one of surrender.

Pullover

CLOTHES RETAIN THE MEMORY OF THOSE WHO ONCE wore them, then one day they cast it off, without warning, with an immediacy typical of material objects. They are guilty of a betrayal that is far worse than anything that men could be accused of. On our bodies we wear undergarments, woollens and furs that are most intimately connected to us, which smell of us and resemble us, and within them we leave the scent of our skin, its olfactory imprint and its breath. I have kept, for instance, an old pullover that my Uncle Dédé wore when he used to come to work at our house. A ten-hour day, side by side, amid the dust, rubble, plaster, grout, Gauloises and the beers that were shared. It was the second house in which we had worked in this way. With the first one, there were three of us. My father-in-law, Iaschou, as project manager. My uncle and I did the unskilled work. A happy memory. Iaschou died a few years later. I was waiting for my uncle one morning, preparing the coffee as usual. He didn't come: he had died during the night. His pullover was lying on a stool. Almost human. Weary. With holes here and there. And two small patches of fresh plaster that had become enmeshed in the fibre of the fabric. I buried my face in it as I would in the arms of a beloved person, and wept. My uncle was there, shockingly present in the cold whiff of his cigarette, the lingering traces of some cheap aftershave, the cement dust, the wallpaper paste, rising up through an alchemy subliminally accumulated in the fabric. I can't throw it in the dustbin, or wear it. I put it aside in a cupboard, near the attic, from which I frequently retrieve it so that I can touch it, breathe it in and, thereby, rediscover the uncle I had loved dearly since childhood, who watched me grow up like a second father, though freed of all responsibility and all the worries of fatherhood, and who, as a result, was less demanding and more amusing than my father. To grieve is like tossing a fistful of life at the games death plays. We know that death will only be blinded for a brief instant, but it does us good. And we can carry on. One day, pressing the pullover to my face, I could find nothing of him. Everything had gone. My uncle had departed from it. It was just an old bit of clobber, without memory and without soul. I keep it nevertheless. It's still up there, near the sky, in the cupboard in the attic.

Mustiness

SMALL, TIGHTLY PACKED ROWS OF PUPILS, BENEATH the slanting rain, in the most depressing months of childhood, October, November or March, months without snow, just wringing wet, and cold. The Wednesday afternoon boarders' walk is cancelled when the driving rain lashes down over the Lunévillois. So I won't be able to walk to Jolivet, Chanteheux, La Petite Fourasse or Méhoncourt, and enjoy a little of the countryside, the fields, the twists and turns of the river that allow me to daydream, or see the black-and-white hides of the cows, their udders full of warm milk, and sniff the open barns filled with hay and straw. I will be unable to see, in the distance, the blue trapezium of the Donon, standing out from the chain of the Vosges hills, which is an emotional compass for me, through which I can discern my origins, and which soothes and delights me. We leave the boarding school under the kindly gaze of M. Chapotot. The supervisor takes us to the public library, hard by the sandstone towers of Saint-Jacques church:

we spend just over three hours there, I reckon Jean-Christophe Vaimbois, nicknamed Nichon, the tit, who would choose to end his life at the age of nineteen, Hervé Lelièvre, Yannick Wein, and the others. Heads bowed, reading or dozing, it all depends. In a silence that is even more muffled due to the early dusk glazing the reading room in grey light. A wide, unvarnished floor. On the walls, the books, large and small, ancient or modern, are packed against each other like timid neighbours. I read until my eyes are drooping. The clock stands still. Time and place no longer exist. I turn over the pages with their smell of old paper and fresh ink, book jackets covered in dust, specks of which flurry about under the beam of the lights; that damp smell, too, of heavy and rarely touched works that seem to resent being opened and suppurate minuscule tears. No doubt it was here, in this old-fashioned library, deep in silence, among the absent faces of my classmates and their listless bodies, intoxicated by the *remugle*, the mustiness – for that is the name of the smell of old books, as I learned much later – that I entered a realm, that of fiction and its myriad paths, that I have never really left. I resemble books. I reside in books. They are the places I inhabit, both as reader and author, and which best define me.

Waking up

I WAKE FROM THE NIGHT, ASTONISHED AT LIFE. AS time goes by, I think of this ordinary moment as a precarious, reoccurring reprieve. I'm frightened that it might cease, and that one night, at bedtime, while switching off the light and giving a kiss to the one I love, I might, without realising, be carrying out these familiar gestures for the last time. It's nothing to do with a fear of dying, but rather a dread of no longer being alive, that is to say setting off on my own along unknown paths, be they those of death, which no-one can comprehend, but which I visualise as a blind alley which my ineffective senses and my irreversibly dimmed conscience will be unable to explain to me, or be they those of life, a life shorn, however, of the presence of my beloved, and which would therefore be a lame existence, cut off in its prime, and tinged with blood. And so when I wake and gradually take my place once more in the slowly rousing world, in the dawning light, and my hands, as though magnetised, start to stroke the body that lies next to mine, and I feel the warmth of this body, its slow, rhythmical breathing – for it may still be asleep – never suspecting that I have reluctantly woken, I snuggle up as close as I can, flesh against flesh, imbibing the nocturnal warmth enmeshed in the fabric of the sheets and that lighter, thinner material of the nightdress she wears, leaving her shoulders bare, as well as her arms and her cleavage, over which my fingers wander in search of life and her throbbing pulse. These are moments of the greatest intimacy and of love that needs no word to describe it. The scents of bodies that love one another, though separated by solitary slumber during the hours of the night, are like those that float through fairy tales in which princesses trapped in an everlasting sleep await the prince's kiss. What I inhale is the warmth of life in hibernation, filled with a restfulness that has soothed the body and relaxed it, like a length of soft silk released from a drawer. Before my beloved opens her eyes, before she even sees me or smiles at me, what I want to cling to as I inhale her skin and her hair, is our presence together that turns this awakening into a new beginning for our love, the risen dawn of an enduring harmony.

Rivers

WITH OUR BARE FEET ON THE EDGE OF THE WEIR, we are gazing down over the waterfall, happy little fellows surrounded by churning waves. Our 10-speed Randonneurs Peugeot cross-country bikes are waiting for us, doubly padlocked to the railings of the electricity transformer. The River Meurthe flows upstream like a sated boa constrictor, slow, obese, spread out between the banks of the Digue and the Île aux Corbeaux. Deep. And you can imagine all those *noyés pensifs* intent on drowning themselves, dragging their troubles over the two stretches of water. Then there's the strange concrete structure, a sort of gentle slide, as wide as a bed and about thirty metres long. The waves flow swiftly along it at no great depth – they barely lap our calves – trailing long streams of green mosses that lend the now transparent waters the sparkle of a mountain stream. We fish amid the deafening noise of the frothing foam that casts back at us a gentle spray cut with smells of silt and warm water. A massive wash.

Niagara. Zambezi. Adventure within the reach of a bicycle ride, and in the evening, our net full of bream, *boucsés* and bleaks from the depths, we return home with our spoils, proud and exhausted, as though the survival of our families depended on them. A land of rivers, both rushing and trickling. Rivers, canals, ponds and small lakes surround and criss-cross my town, and once upon a time they would flood it regularly at the end of each winter, coursing down rue du Saulcy Pitou, where my Aunt Paulette lived, sending silt-laden surges along rue du Moulin upon which people who owned boats reached their houses. Some great characters are associated in my memory with every location. Père Frache, with his Popeye face, who taught me about the River Sânon; Mesdames Gye and Pauly – the only fisherwomen in Dombasle – who told me about the River Poncé; Père Bergé, the Grand Canal; Père Idon, the Petit Canal and the subtle technique of fishing with hempseed; and my Uncle Dédé, the bends of the Meurthe. Fishing is a matter of patience and interpretation. Before casting your rod, it is advisable to know how to fathom the water, to sniff it and take its pulse, gauge its depth, its snares and hazards. I am a lover who has no lack of mistresses. I could name them blindfolded just from the smell of their breaths. Sludge and a stench of gas oil for the canal from the Marne to the Rhine; dried reeds, miasmas of sewage and black mud for the Poncé; the fleeting, green freshness of the Grand Canal; the earthy oozing of the Sânon over its high clay banks; the languor of the Meurthe, at times sugary, at times brackish, where nearby the glasswort grows, which we eat raw. I love the blending of the countryside and the water. Rivers soothe and transport me. Daydreaming about water is probably the kind of reverie that best suits my superficial nature, for I've never really been able to come to terms with myself. I also remember my joy at living for a while in towns encircled by loops in rivers: Fumay in the Ardennes, a dead city and a former slate-quarry centre, with forests that are ringed by the Meuse; Besançon, which is wedded to the Doubs; Strasbourg and the fast-flowing Ill. Perhaps in my case it is to do with some bygone memory of obsidional fears that, paradoxically, makes me appreciate those natural defences, those rolling moats, rich with fish, within which the city believes it sleeps in peace. I also think, from having verified it on numerous occasions, that however unassuming, this river and these streams, through the sudden gusts that rise up from their current, are able to bring me news from home when I've been away for a time. These are unsettling moments when the realities of memory and of the present become jumbled up, when I am ageless and I become the plaything of this newly activated sense, and I simultaneously regret that I am there and yet feel glad that, a thousand miles from my birthplace, I can recognise fragments of its aromas and, like a patient archaeologist with scraps of pottery, can piece together broken bits of my old everyday life.

Classroom

THE INK ON OUR FINGERS LEAVES MESSY FINGER-prints, which, at playtime, are diluted by the cold water tap into bluish pools on the cement playground. We write with the tips of our tongues stuck between our lips, hunched up in our smocks that shrink by the month, our elbows flat on our desks, our pens sweetened by saliva, gliding over the squared paper. Upstrokes and downstrokes. The motion and the concentration are those of a copyist from the Middle Ages. Chalk, smock, slate-board, Sergeant-Major writing-pen, pink blotting paper, ceramic inkwell that fits neatly into the top of the wooden desk. And in the way of primary school mythology we become perfect models for Robert Doisneau-style weekend photographers, as we drunkenly inhale and sometimes eat the smooth white glue with its smell of fresh almonds. Monsieur François elegantly smokes cigarettes as he sweeps his right hand through his silvery hair. He adopts a regal pose when he calls us to the blackboard to interrogate us. I feel terrified, even when I know the answers. It's a fear such as I have never experienced subsequently, except perhaps a little later on, in third year, with Monsieur Gueutal, the maths teacher, who never smiles and has a peculiarly Nazi face, white, almost shaven hair and unbearable steely eyes that are a bit like Laurence Olivier's in "Marathon Man", although in actual fact he's probably a very decent man outside school hours. When we hesitate, Monsieur François gets to his feet and comes over to us. With his fingers, he grabs hold of the delicate hairs that grow beneath one's temple and the more serious the mistake the harder he tugs. Pain. A pain that continues and grows worse. You try to stand on tiptoe so that it hurts less. You feel you want to disappear. The classroom floor is made of thick planks that are washed each week in water mixed with disinfectant. A pale, worn wood scored by the shoes of generations of pupils. In its grain it retains the stench of chlorine, while at the same time trying to remind us of its origins by exuding faint fragrances of ligneous fibres, like an almost vanished olfactory echo of the tree it once belonged to. Whenever I happen to come across similar floors in other places, remote village cafés or parish halls, instinctively, even today, I can feel myself rising up on tiptoe and my fingers reaching to soothe my temples.

Fir tree

IT IS SAID OF SOMEONE FROM THE VOSGES, SO AS to poke fun at his taciturn nature and brusque manner, that he is half man and half fir tree. When I'm far from fir tree forests, I live as if in slow motion. It's as though my roots have been severed. I miss the trees' constant vitality, their spreading fullness, their glowing scent of resin and their harmless needles. Before the war, my father was a woodcutter, a farmer and a worker in the chemical industry. After the war, he became a policeman, but he never forgot his forests. The house where he was born is embedded in one. Dark woods that rise in a slope as far as the Soye rock, the ruins of Pierre-Percée castle and the Chapelotte pass, where so many battles took place during the First World War that scars can still be seen. He worked felling in the valley of the Plaine, a river where trout and minnows are plentiful, beside which an old Roman road runs, overlooked by the Donon, a sandstone temple celebrating the cult of Velleda on its summit. It is one of the places with more conifers than anywhere else in France. You can't escape fir trees both old and young, dark and huge, and possessed of an almost Carolingian majesty, or the spruces clustered in groups all along the footpaths. Picnic. We fill the 4.L. Renault with baskets, rugs, folding chairs, camping stoves, salad bowls, pétanque balls and badminton rackets. We don't go very far. We go back to a haunt of my childhood, by a small stream in the middle of the forest that we reach via a sandy pink path. Our spot. The sun has been driven behind the branches. In the shade it smells of sap and moss. Your fingers turn blue in the stream if you leave them there for too long. The beer and the wine are soon cooled. Uncle Dédé and Aunt Jeanine often come with us, as does my other aunt, Paulette, whom I've always known as a widow, her husband Nénesse having died before I was born, electrocuted in the salt factory. In photographs with crinkled edges, we pose, seated around a camping table. Smiles, vests and full bellies. The fir trees envelop us with their low branches. It's a world of tranquillity, of buzzing bees, slow-moving slugs, pharaonic anthills, jays that dart off in a bluish flash, sometimes leaving behind a white feather, tinged with grey, which I stick in my hair. I search for mosses, which even in the heat of the summer always retain a little moisture, a peaty sponginess. Sometimes I dig up small clumps of them and lay them on my thighs. I can get dirty here, roll in the ferns, make myself up by smearing my cheeks with leaf mould that smells of heather roots. I'm allowed to. I hug the trunks of the fir trees. The palms of my hands get sticky with a resin that looks like teardrops. I pull off crystals that smell sweetly of throat pastilles and which cluster around the trunks' wounds. Woodpeckers have drilled into them with their mean beaks. Green woodpeckers, great spotted woodpeckers that we nickname "red arses", large excavating birds. Time stands still. I can hear the laughter of adults digesting. I eat whatever I can find, beechnuts, wild raspberries, blueberries, blackberries, young shoots. I should like to be a deer. On the way back, I fall asleep in the car, enveloped in my dreams of animals and wrapped in a rug on which, days later, fir needles and grains of sand can still be found.

Tomato sauce

We live on provisions. The gardens supply us with vegetables, the orchards with fruit. The hutches and the farmyard, meat and eggs. The rest is purchased two or three times a year, in huge quantities: half a pig, which we cut up, salt, smoke, freeze, and reduce to sausages, brawn and black puddings; and then sugar, rice, lentils, pasta, as though a war were imminent. Stockpiling is an act of survival, an instinctive reaction here in Lorraine, the doormat of Europe, over which, at one time or another, all the armies have wiped their boots or their arses. We eat fresh food in season, and from jars the rest of the year. Le Parfait jars. All lined up on the cellar shelves. A static parade. Standing perfectly to attention. These transparent urns display their entrails of peas, beans, carrots, jellied rabbit or chicken, turnips, sauerkraut, broad beans, gherkins, cherries, redcurrants, raspberries, tomato sauce. Summer toil: pick, prepare, that is to say, where appropriate, top and tail, remove the stalk, slice, squeeze, stone, peel, cook. Out of the dry earth, which looks arid and thin on top, huge tangles of greenery rise up, supported, in the case of the beans, by long sticks that we call *rames*. Further down, the Lilliputian forest of tomato plants. Further still, creeping along and weighed down, are the marrows, the pumpkins, the squashes. The hosing duties, carried out at both dawn and dusk, reveal the intimacy involved in growing crops; it's as if they had been sprayed naked by us and the water spread over their bodies has become impregnated with their aromas. The tomato plants, for example, exhibit a pungent flair – in a flash you are in a Provençal priest's garden – whereas lettuces emit a fragile freshness; gherkins, a spicy and proletarian scent; the leaves of beans, a jungle-like mugginess. Maturation. The turgescent tomatoes, split in places by the thrust of their flesh, bulging, cyst-like, magnificently variable, are laid in wicker baskets. In the yard behind the house, in the cool shade facing north, my father brings out a large burner, which he places on the ground and attaches to a gas canister. My mother washes tin saucepans that are so big they could cook me in them. I survey the scene, leaning out of the open window in our kitchen. An Aztec massacre: my mother's hands are bloody. Her knife slices, crushes, separates, extracts the pulp, exposing pips, flesh and alveoli. The tomatoes weep their juice. It makes me think of a jam into which I long to plunge my arms. The saucepans are full. They all whisper, bubble, chatter and boil. My mother stirs with a wooden spoon, puts her finger in to taste, adds seasoning and sings "Que sera sera". My father accompanies her, whistling, and sets up the steriliser, a kind of boiler, made of zinc, that looks like a top hat worn by a giant at a fairground. Very soon the tomatoes have disappeared. All that is left is their mingled blood, glossy, smooth and piping hot, the smell of which rises up to me, casting its spell. Sugar and sunshine. The essence of summer. Using a ladle, my mother fills the jars as my father hands them to her, then he puts a rubber ring around their neck, closes them and places them in the steriliser. A buzzard wheels mathematically above our heads, seeking a theorem of the circle. Later on, I shall play with the hose and create rainbows. Later on, I shall go fishing. Later on, when I get home, I shall lick the still warm saucepans. Later on, "Que sera sera"!

Soap

A PERFECT BAR. A LARGE ANIMAL'S TOOTH DROPPED from an extinct jawbone, which deposits some of its enamel and pulp beneath the nails that scratch it. Elusive, slippery, escaping into the water of the communal washtub it has already streaked a milky colour. The women chatter. They are old, their yellow and grey hair held in a bun. Old, as all women are when you're a child, but older still are those who were born at the beginning of the century, the twentieth, and have spent their lives encircled by the bloody tyranny of wars. The place has a smell of the bath-house, and the occasional transparent bubble that is formed by the whacks of the beetle, and which I burst immediately. For I am in the water, a small human fish, watched over by the washerwomen who are splashing me. They wring the sheets with their hands. They wipe the sweat from their foreheads. They laugh, they jabber away, they gossip without interrupting their work. I don't know how to swim. My bare feet are perched on the floor of the *lavoir* or wash-house. I can't see them. I can't see my body. It has been swallowed up by the soap, which has melted in the water. And the simple, elemental smell, slightly cold and almost clinical, fills my body, as though it were washing it as well. My grandmother takes me out of the water. She lifts me effortlessly. I don't weigh a thing. I am still just a small human creature and she dries me with the loose tail of her blue smock. I shiver. My skin grows taut and starts to quiver. I breathe in my new smell. I have become the soap. Grandmother dresses me. I rush outside, into the sunshine. I screw up my eyes. I let the heat of the day cloak me. The Pont de Voleurs is over there, so narrow that two men on foot cannot pass one another. Through a cast-iron pipe, the water from the *lavoir* meets the waters of the Sânon at this spot. A long whitish trail like a Milky Way, remorselessly churning its galaxies into the swirl. An object of endless liquid curiosity to the astonished tiny alevins that plunge into it and frolic there in uncontrollable and gleeful sinewy movements, before dying, sprigs of lifeless scales carried away by the current.

Le sexe féminin

WHAT DO MOST BOYS DREAM ABOUT WHEN THEY watch girls go by? Of that, of course. Our humanity is dual, made up of two equal mysteries that observe one another, skirt one another, and intertwine without being altered in any way, or very little. Our bodies, which can at times be merged, cannot however be mistaken for one another. The theory of the humours of antiquity that man is warm and ardent, while woman is moist and cold, is certainly incorrect, though pleasingly poetic. From the moment I attended nursery school, I wanted to know about girls' sexual parts and I would make up games and forfeits in order to be able to slip a hand into my classmates' cotton knickers. My five-year-old self seemed to be caressing strange soft bulges, slit in the middle by a velvety vertical line, the frontier to a land beyond whose bounds, either out of prudence or perhaps fear, I preferred not to venture further. Joëlle, Christine, Véronique, sensual companions who smelled of Nivea cream, of warm skin, and of the washing powder used by their mothers, Paic, Coral, Ariel. After which, there is a great void. Modesty – not so much my own as that of my girlfriends – as well as the separation that primary school imposes between boys and girls, distances us from one another. High school brings us together again, but we have changed. We boys show off and play rough games, while the girls stand in small circles in the playground, whispering and giving us mocking glances. "To smell like a girl" becomes an insult for us and we spread jokes, which we have naturally never verified, about the olfactory affinity of their sexual organs with the smell of seafood, of rotten fish, of pink or grey prawns. An aversion that is paraded and flaunted, particularly when we learn, without really understanding, that from time to time streams of thick blood soil their crotches, flowing from that cleft of which we only have a very vague memory. Sabine has an orange swimsuit she has never worn before. On our first joint swimming pool outing. Boys and girls looking at one another, trying to imagine the shapes of each other's bodies. We are showing off a little less. We boys retain our immature bodies, whereas the breasts of many of the girls are swelling and stretching. Diving in, climbing out again, one after the other. Sabine dives in and emerges from the water. Her wet swimming costume is no longer orange. It has become transparent. Just above her thighs, like some cabalistic sign, a black triangle has appeared. She notices it and, embarrassed, puts both her hands over it. Too late. My jaw drops. Stupefaction. We remember the precise moment when vocations are born. Even today, I can recall it quite clearly. It has guided a quest that has never exhausted its delights. Nerval and Gautier roamed Europe in the *pourchas du blond*, in pursuit of the fair. I spent years discovering women's sexual organs. Not so much in a search for their origins, nor so as to assess what Paul Claudel describes in an appallingly cynegetic phrase that makes me think that he neither loved, nor respected, nor really knew them, as *le terrier de la race*, the burrow of the species, but so as to marvel at the subtleties of their shape, softness and smell. For no genitals resemble any other, none are embellished with the same fragrances, and the kisses that are laid there, like offerings or solaces, try to subdue the beautiful sleeping creature who appears to dwell there with a fertile scent which, depending on different women, is reminiscent of cedar wood, toasted bread, the faint acidity of citron, the musk of certain wild animal furs, milk, malt, caramel; yet all this in a fading of notes, a soughing of perfume, which, if they are to be truly experienced and celebrated, require one to get as close as possible, to press one's lips and nostrils there, to kiss and breathe in, eyes closed, with the kneeling tribute of the worshipper before the goddess. Fingers and lips that hover over a woman retain the memory of their scent for a long, long time, as if it did not wish to die, just as we ourselves do not wish to die except, perhaps, as in the most beautiful of dreams, within the very hollow of their thighs.

Sewage works

WE DON'T STEP OVER WASTE WATER ANYMORE. THE *saute-ruisseau* (the "skip-kennel", or, literally, "gutter-hopper") has disappeared. He survives barely in a few of Balzac's novels. May he rest in peace. A term has died. The sewer has got the better of him. The sewer. The sewer which, incidentally, was invented as much for hygiene as for the mind: striving for salubrity, it also encouraged hypocrisy, for we enjoy making things disappear. Lying to ourselves. We produce ever more refuse, but we slip it under the carpet. Waste water. Dirty, murky, contaminated, rancid, muddy. Witnesses for the prosecution. Our lives may be read in slurry, but when will the trial be? The city comforts itself with its great network of pipes and ejects its shaming waters – which it turns its back on while holding its nose – far beyond its boundaries, into open vats. Swimming pools without swimmers or swimming instructors. Open to the sky. Surrounded by pretty, well-kept lawns. In the sewage treatment plant, they purify and clarify using procedures of which the simple mortal is ignorant. He can barely see through the wire fencing – though the curious onlooker is rare here – the sludge stirring as though it were the must of fermenting grapes. The colours deter the most intrepid of onlookers: lumpy brown, sickly beige, diarrhoeal ochre, intestinal grey. A disturbing pathological palette, as though the essential prognosis of an entire people were involved. You might think that it smelled. Well, no. Just as you cannot judge a book by its cover, you cannot judge a smell by its colour. You have to be able to discern the soul of the Beauty beneath the features of the Beast. Who can do this? All of us if we really allow ourselves. Consider a lagoon. Walls lapped for centuries by hybrid water, half-fresh, half-salt. The eroded foundations of decrepit *palazzi* with Moorish windows. Moss-covered bridges. Brick embankments that have become sponge-like over time, like bones grown soft. Mooring posts painted and repainted by tides and algae, the *acqua alta* of November that floods the uneven paving stones of *piazze* and landing stages; the Visconti-like heat of August that gilds adolescent skins, mothers' smiles, the Lido, and sates itself on the very canals by drinking them at night, the mists, winds, seabirds, resident pigeons. *Chiese, vaporetti*. A small stage for a permanent display. A decadence that endures, and thus escapes decay. The Venetian States created an embassy in each foreign land. They were ubiquitous. La Serenissima, which likes to throw her gold around in fistfuls so that one should remember her and sometimes die because of her, has not skimped: each of her sewage works is a secret legation. One just has to know this. They issue passports and visas to all connoisseurs, without delay or charging a fee. At all seasons, without staff. How many times, at the edge of my own Petit Canal, have I stopped by the waste-water tanks and breathed in Venice. And how many times, wandering along the Grand Canal of the City of the Doges or walking along its alleys, have I thought of the sewage works at Dombasle, and therefore of my own small town, and my own small region, *qui m'est une province, et beaucoup d'avantage* ["which is a province to me and much more besides", Joachim du Bellay]? Geography, which is a very ancient science, can also be mischievous. It plays with us by playing games with itself. It shuffles places in the way that one shuffles cards. Queens come face to face with knaves. They then become confused, lower their gaze, breathe in their fragrances and dream. Queens let them be since, ultimately, what does the future hold? Who shall be King tomorrow? Who shall no longer be anything?

Earth

I LIKE DIGGING HOLES. I LIKE HIDING IN THEM.
It's a spring or autumn pastime. In summer, I prefer fishing,
and the earth is too dry and hard in any case. It would spurn
me. I could only scratch at it, no more. March or November.
Sated months. The earth is heavy and the water has lain there
long enough for it to be dug up. I have my tools. My hands first
and foremost. Some spades too, shovels, pickaxes, mining
rods. I dig. In our garden, before any sowing and after any
picking. In Bernardo Bertolucci's "1900", the two boys stick
their small willies into the field-mice holes and one of them
says that in this way he is "fucking the earth". I want to bury
all of myself in it. Disappear into it. Not to die, no, but hide
there for a while. Get to know it. Enter its womb. Make myself
a shelter there. The earth in our gardens is black and less
compact than the red clay of the Rambêtant or the banks of
the Sânon. It yields, it offers no resistance. I come across a
few bits of broken crockery there, the bowl of a clay pipe, some

pebbles, part of a bayonet from the 1870 war – the one fought by the Uhlans at Rezonville and Gravelotte – and some rats' bones. I dig for hours, enveloped in the stench of entrails. I smell my hands frequently, and the sides of the hole in which I am slowly burying myself. Sometimes, I even taste this earth, before spitting it out again and I feel it on my tongue for a long time afterwards, the particles and seeds, the taste of comingled metals between my teeth. My task achieved, I remain in my hole. I can sit myself down, my knees drawn up against my chest, with a few provisions, two bars of chocolate, a hunk of bread, a flask of water. I don't get bored. I'm at peace. I am inside my hole. Much later, I shall read "The Burrow" by Franz Kafka. But in my case I'm really alone. Nothing else is digging alongside me. I'm not frightened of my neighbour. One day, I manage to dig a hole far deeper than the previous ones and I stay there, overwhelmed by this excavation that has surpassed all my hopes. I feel happy and relatively warm. The earth retains the heat of my body. I think of moles, of their thick fur, their hard feet. Blind creatures, condemned to dig. A life of tunnels and perpetual darkness. My father traps them with fine metal jaws that he places over their holes. The walls of my hole collapse without warning. I am buried. Fortunately, the layer of earth is not too thick. I don't die from suffocation. I'm not frightened either. I've got earth everywhere, in my hair, on my face. It's managed to run down my collar and slip between my skin and my clothing. Revenge. A shower of earth. A black earth that smells of cold, rotted roots and decomposition, and a bit like gas too, just as truffles do, which are the diamonds of the darkness. I don't want to be cremated. I'm afraid of fire. I'm frightened that the fire will metabolise me at the beginning of the combustion into an ordinary piece of grilled meat. I don't want to smell of barbecue. I'm not a rib of beef. And then the ashes, they don't do anything with them. Urns are ridiculous. Often ugly. The whole of this large body in there? No, thank you. A columbarium looks like a cemetery for dogs. I want to be put into a hole for one last time. I'd willingly do it myself, but I'd be taken for a madman. I want to be buried in Dombasle, right opposite my childhood home, not very far from our garden. Among the landscape of the Rambêtant and the Sânon. Last wishes. The earth is the same on both sides of the road. Black and smelling of vegetable gardens and good old dampness. I've seen enough open graves and made enough holes to be certain of this: digging is learning to die.

Lime blossom

IN A PANTOUM FROM LES FLEURS DU MAL, BAUDELAIRE describes the entrancing musical, alchemical and sensory process that dusk generates:

> Voici venir les temps où, vibrant sur sa tige
> Chaque fleur s'évapore ainsi qu'un encensoir;
> Les sons et les parfums vibrent dans l'air du soir;
> Valse mélancolique et langoureux vertige!*

Near the cemetery, on the other side of the Sommerviller road, opposite our house, stands a two-hundred-year-old tree that we call "The Big Lime". I grew up in the shade of its broad and lordly boughs, admiring its twisted, gaunt arborescence, Breughel-like or romantic during the winter months; and in summer, leafy, mossy and humming with the chatter of scores of birds as they pursue one another, make love and lay their eggs. A streetlight serves as its bedside light, illuminating its

* Now is the time when, quivering on its stem, / Each flower exhales its vapour like a censer; / Sounds and scents hover in the evening air; / Melancholy waltz and languid light-headedness!

jade foliage on spring nights with candlelight. The oneiric scene is like a painting by René Magritte or André Delvaux, and at any moment you almost expect to see, in the soft halo that marks out an oblong stretch of pavement from the encircling shadows, a sombrely dressed character wearing a bowler hat, or else a girl with large, almond eyes, diaphanous, and enveloped in long, flimsy veils. May bugs spring to life in this light that for them is sometimes fatal and, given permission to stay up a little longer than usual, we are on the point of capturing them when they fall and crash to the ground, lying there, vulnerable and concussed, for a few seconds. We hold them in our hands and feel the pleasant scratching of their legs on our palms and the hardness of their varnished chitin shells. Later on, the following day, we shall use them in cruel games when they will be transformed into aeroplanes with a circular flight, held by sewing thread. But for the time being, beneath the blossom of "The Big Lime", which is covered in swarms of bees that refuse to go and sleep in their hive, it is hunting season. Above our heads, the tree unfurls its vast umbrella of new leaves, pale petals and floury, dull yellow pollen. Inhaling the scent, we are already gorging ourselves with future honey – as if in a transmutation of matter, with the gas becoming the solid. For these wonderful golden June evenings will be prolonged into snowy and icy December, spread over slices of warm bread on our return from tobogganing, and in the scalding tisane in which the blossoms from the tree, freed from withering in a glass jar, will, through the miracle of instant rehydration, open up again in the hot water, exuding, as a votive tribute, their preserved aromas.

Coffee-roasting

ON ARRIVING IN NANCY, I RENT A FLAT AT 27 GRANDE Rue, in the oldest part of the city. I'm nineteen years old. It's September 1981. Everything there is still grimy and dirty, and home to large, poverty-stricken families, often Portuguese. The cats practise free love and reproduce shamelessly in the shadow of the church of Saint-Epvre. The younger whores frequent place Malval, while the older ones entertain in their bedrooms, in particular Madame Aïda, whom I chat to but no more than that. I've left home and the boarding school at Lunéville, my baccalaureate in my pocket. I enrol at the university, which I frequent very little. I roam around the bars, the bistros, the cafés and the restaurants. My day begins early, at the Excelsior, and ends very late in the evening at this same Excelsior. But in between I have patronised the Deux Hémisphères, the Bar du Lycée, the Institut, the Ch'timi, the Aca, the Carnot, the Foy, the Commerce, the Ducs, the Bar du Marché, the Grand Sérieux, Chez Josy, the café de la Pépinière, the Ecluse, and I'm forgetting many of them. I drink. I dream. Black coffees, brown ales, glasses of red wine, grogs, Picons, tea, orgeat syrup, neat gins. My wages are spent on this. I think of myself as a poet and I write bad verse in spiral-bound notebooks. During the daytime, I read Giacomo Casanova's *Histoire de ma vie* in the very beautiful wood-panelled room at the local library. The volumes in the Pléiade edition are a soft blue. I look at the faces of the studious young girls opposite me, and, in the street, women's bodies. Sometimes, I follow one of them for hours and I try to imagine what her life is like. Occasionally, I may well end up sleeping with her, but that's not my main purpose. I lead this drifting existence for two years. My job as a supervisor in a lycée provides me with a little money and a lot of free time. I'm unhappy, but I don't know I am. I aspire to the life of a *rastaquouère,** but I'm not brave enough. I should like to have a gun in each pocket, even though I don't know how to shoot. You can have the spirit of a bandit, but not the guts. I am an artist without any art. I could end up a drunkard, or a thief, or a pimp, or a professional layabout. I even try to sell counterfeit perfumes by responding to an advertisement. The meeting is arranged in the street where I live, but at the far end, in the more crowded part, near the porte de la Craffe. I climb the stairs of a rickety building. On the third floor, the door opens. I find myself standing in front of someone like me, twenty years on: a scrawny and shifty-looking man, ill at ease in his viscose suit that has a

* A slang term formerly used to describe a gaudy and wealthy foreigner. [Tr.]

stain on the right lapel. Fiddling with his tie and avoiding my gaze, the pathetic crook explains that there's nothing illegal about my future activity, even though it's not exactly approved of either. He hands me a box containing forty samples that are supposed to replicate the best-known eaux de toilette of the time. I must never mention the models or the fraudulent brands. I should make the customers guess them, not name them myself, because it's at that point that my actions could be construed as criminal. He wishes me good luck and tucks away in his trouser pocket the 100 francs surety that he has demanded from me. I find myself outside, one "Corneille" banknote the poorer, with a box of scents under my arm. I feel very stupid all of a sudden. It's a spring morning. The road-sweeping machine has just washed the pavement and cleaned the gutter. The air is still fresh. The blue sky creates cut-out shapes above the grey slate roofs. From the open door of a nearby shop comes a whiff of coffee beans being roasted. Warm, sensual, powerfully immediate. I can't drag myself away. I am bewitched by the smell of these coffee beans, rolling in the scorching metal pan, but also terror-stricken by the scene in the crumbling office I've just described. I've no regrets about my 100 francs, quite the reverse. Some people, as they lie down on a couch, lay down the same sum every week, and do so for years, in order to know themselves a little better. I've simply done a crash course in self-analysis. The truth strikes me all too clearly. The swindler has ripped me off, but he has also, unwittingly, opened my eyes: I am nothing but an idiot who has driven straight into a brick wall. I waste my time on trifling, worthless things. I am nothing much and very soon I'm going to be nothing at all. In this morning's beautiful, ancient light, awash with sunshine, I loiter on the pavement for a long time, enveloped by the smell of roasted coffee mingling with the fresh air, my box of fake perfumes under my arm, bereft of great expectations, but enriched once more by a lively clear-headedness, and chastened and warned off, with a few harmless kicks in the arse, from a life that can never be mine.

Turtledoves

THE WAGUETTE TWINS LIVE IN A LARGE HOUSE WITH a simple façade looking onto rue Gabriel Péri, the Champs Elysées of Dombasle, but where you can wander around in a vest or in worker's overalls. It's the property of their grandfather, Père Resling, a retired seed merchant, who wears a beret and a moustache, and has a quavering voice and a bent back. An icon. He drives around in an ancient Citroën 2C.V. or on a Vélosolex moped. In short, the ideal grandfather, and the sort I dream of, never having known either of my own. Behind the house, there is a garden and extensive, uncultivated grounds with ancient trees whose branches spread as far as the Cités Elisa, and the Clinique Jeanne d'Arc, where I was born one February day. Summer and autumn, this vast garden witnesses us laughing, growing up, hiding from one another, fighting and caking each other in mud. We run around, sleep and build fires there, far from the adults and their solemn ways. When we are about thirteen, one of the two Waguettes,

Laurent, begins breeding turtledoves in a lean-to shed. The pairs and their offspring proliferate. When you went inside you were hit by a polite whiff of excrement that was scarcely visible, a delicate smell of straw and feathers, of stagnant water, of seeds and warm down. An avian aristocracy. One that has nothing in common with the coarse stench of our chicken-run – which I adore for all that – and which is a sort of local housing scheme accommodating an endless succession of lodgers unconcerned about cleanliness, who leave shit and large feathers everywhere, but also, as though to make up for the disorder, some very good eggs. The turtledove is a regal bird. She lays eggs and lives elegantly. In high season, the broods abound, and beneath the mothers' warm bellies we finger the fragile eggs in which the filaments of life are developing. The beams of sunlight give the hut the feeling of a chapel reverberating with cooing. Some very delicate stray feathers flutter about in the mirages. Dark eyes consider us, protruding from grey dresses adorned with slender black necklaces. We feel a little ashamed, I think, to be rummaging like this through family histories that are not our own.

Old age

IF THEIR CHEEKS RESEMBLE CERTAIN FRUITS, APPLES or pears, that are specked and withered from being left for too long in a china fruit bowl, they also have a waxen, faded, charming, sweet and distant smell, the memory of a fragrance rather than the fragrance itself. Death, which is never very far away, lends the body a moving, eroded appearance like that of a fine linen material – washed many times, worn many times – the almost translucent thread of which has a perfect smoothness, fragile though it is. The skin, the hair and the fingers of elderly people are like a fabric that we want to keep for ever and which we look after carefully so that it can never be torn. Yet we know that soon we won't be able to embrace these creatures with their hesitant, delicate ways and that is why, at every reunion or farewell occasion, the kisses we bestow on them, and those they give us in return, are filled with a heightened emotion because we desperately want to retain everything about them, the slightest smile or wink, the words, the caresses, the warmth, the smell. In my childhood, I remember old ladies whose faces were scattered with cysts – we called them "cherries" – whose chins were prolonged with wispy greying beards, and whose facial features scarcely invited affection, but who, if you moved close to them, exuded scents of almond milk, orange flowers and old roses. There is such a gulf between the repellent appearance of their faces and their broken bodies – some bent and walking at right angles – and the fragrances associated with young girls and even babies in their cradles, that I often think I am dreaming these smells. But I also remember another old woman, a garden witch, who used to pee standing up, without lifting her long skirts or her apron, her clouded, milky eyes gazing into the distance as she clutched her spade, and then got on with her task having relieved herself. Whenever I pass her in the streets, pulling her cart which contains her tools and whatever crop she has picked, I quicken my step, not because the stench of rancid urine that still pervades her clothes might cause me to faint, but simply because she frightens me; I'm still at that indeterminate age which, while distancing us from a kind of primitive thinking, retains the most vivid superstitions. I must also mention some of the old men of that period, whose company I often seek in order to compensate for the absence of my own grandfathers, both of whom died years before I was born – in 1938, from leukaemia, in the case of my father's father, Lucien; in 1957, from a cardiac arrest in the street, in the case of my mother's father, Paul. He died from an "attack", to use the word I hear constantly in my childhood, one that describes only too well the violence that death exacts, the ghastly savagery with which it surprises its victim. I like old men. I like everything about them. Their expressions, their words, their gestures, their worn-out bicycles, their *mobylettes*, their bad temper, their knowledge. The clothes they wear, summer and winter, the patched-up brown or burgundy-coloured woollen jumpers, the overalls whose shininess softens into the colour of faded beach canvas, the berets basques with their inner leather band that has cracked from imbibing so much sweat. And the way of life in the numerous cafés of Dombasle which has seasoned them with an added whiff of caporal tobacco, of leather pouches, cheap red wine, widowerhood, engine oil and bonfires. My father smells like that during the last years of his life, though less so of tobacco since he does not smoke. And we who have never embraced one another previously very much – my father never displayed any form of affection – make up for lost time. I like to hold him in my arms when I come to visit him or say goodbye to him, and I make the moment last. His body has become weak and scrawny. Where once muscles and fat formed compact masses, his shoulder-blades are now close together. I clasp him to me. I kiss him several times. I have the heartrending impression that I am embracing and smelling a very old child.

Travels

BAUDELAIRE – YET AGAIN – UNDERSTOOD THAT
worlds may be contained in bottles, or among the drowsy locks
of a sleeping head of hair. And I always take his poems with
me, like a vade mecum that's better than any travel guide, or
guidebooks for any journey, because travelling is also about
losing yourself, ridding yourself of the familiar so as to be born
anew, without any reference points, and allowing your senses
to become acquainted with the landscape. To smell, as never
before, the breath of new lands. And thus, over the years, I have
frequently got lost, and happily so, in the markets of Istanbul,
of Marrakesh, of Cairo, Aswan, Taipei, Huaráz, Shanghai, Den-
paser, Bandung, Lima, Saigon, Cho Lon, of Hué or Hanoi,
Malatya, Helsinki, Mérida; of many towns, both large or small,
either baking hot like Diyarbakir, which conceals its tobacco
market of heady, golden heaps in the shade of an old cara-
vanserai, or freezing cold, like Cracow in January, where I search
among markets piled with furs, and cribs made of silver paper

and musk, until the tips of my fingers are numb. The names are poems. The fragrances are vessels that lead us on a gentle meander. Two places lure me whenever I travel and, whatever time I arrive, they are the ones I visit first. The church, if I am in a Christian country, and the market. The church, because I know that I can find the same smell of cold stone, wax, myrrh and incense everywhere. In some ways, it is my portable house, my permanent home on account of its familiar imagery, its peacefulness and its restraint. The market, because I can feel the soul of a country there, the texture of its skin, the fruit of its labour amid a thrilling mingling of odours, both frightful and delicious, of raw or grilled fat, lemongrass, coriander cut roughly with scissors, the droppings of caged birds, the insipid meat of newly killed beasts, jasmine, weather-beaten hides, sulphur, cinnamon, rose petals and entrails, fresh or roasted almonds, camphor, ether and honey, sausages and mint, lilies, oil, soups, doughnuts, cod and octopus, dried seaweed and seeds. To recite their names, to inhale their syllables is to write the great poem of the world and that of its deepest longings. The starving Blaise Cendrars understood this well in his list of imaginary "Menus", written as he shivered in the heart of a New York that rejected him. Each letter has a smell, each verb, a fragrance. Each word disseminates into the memory a place and its exhalations. And the text, which is gradually woven together according to the random combinations of the alphabet and memory, then becomes the wondrous river, a thousand times more ramified and sweet-smelling, of the life we dream of, of the life we have lived, of our life to come, which by turn transports us and exposes us.

I know that I have existed, and being sure of this because I have felt it, I also know that once I have stopped feeling I shall no longer exist.

GIACOMO CASANOVA, *Histoire de ma vie*

TRANSLATOR'S NOTE

I should like to thank Philippe Claudel and his wife Dominique for inviting me to their home in Dombasle and for allowing me to sample just a few of their local parfums.

I also want to express my gratitude to Ben Faccini for his thoughtful editing of my text.

E.C.

PHILIPPE CLAUDEL is a novelist, film director and university lecturer. His film "I've Loved You So Long" won the 2009 BAFTA for Best Film Not in English. He is the author of *Grey Souls*, *Brodeck's Report*, *Monsieur Linh and His Child* and *The Investigation*, and in 2012 was appointed to l'Académie Goncourt.

EUAN CAMERON's translations include works by Julien Green, Simone de Beauvoir and Paul Morand, and biographies of Marcel Proust and Irène Némirovsky.